国家级一流本科课程配套教材

理工学术英语

主　编　杨　玉
副主编　王嫦丽　闫　锋
编　者　王裕森　常丹丹　侯丽梅

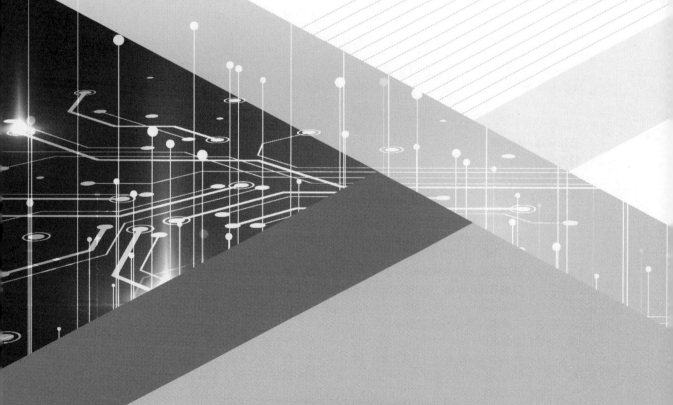

清华大学出版社
北　京

内 容 简 介

本教材主要包括学术英语阅读、写作、听力、交流、词汇、语法和翻译等 7 个单元，既关注学术语篇的宏观结构，也聚焦微观的阅读、听力和写作技巧，并通过系统梳理学术词汇的特点和语法特征，帮助学生掌握学术论文写作的方法、熟练运用翻译技巧进行科技文献翻译。本教材为混合式数字化教材，除配套"理工学术英语"慕课外，书中部分内容和资源均提供二维码，可直接扫码在线查看。本教材另配有 PPT 课件，读者可登录 www.tsinghuaelt.com 下载使用。

本教材适用于本科及以上阶段学生的学术英语课程，也可供对学术英语感兴趣的读者作为阅读材料。

图书在版编目（CIP）数据

理工学术英语 / 杨玉主编. —北京：清华大学出版社，2021.9（2025.1重印）
国家级一流本科课程配套教材
ISBN 978-7-302-58552-7

Ⅰ.①理…　Ⅱ.①杨…　Ⅲ.①理科（教育）—学术交流—英语—高等学校—教材　Ⅳ.① G423.02

中国版本图书馆 CIP 数据核字（2021）第 132314 号

责任编辑：刘　艳
封面设计：子　一
责任校对：王凤芝
责任印制：沈　露

出版发行：清华大学出版社
　　　　网　　址：https://www.tup.com.cn, https://www.wqxuetang.com
　　　　地　　址：北京清华大学学研大厦 A 座　　邮　编：100084
　　　　社 总 机：010–83470000　　邮　购：010–62786544
　　　　投稿与读者服务：010–62776969, c-service@tup.tsinghua.edu.cn
　　　　质量反馈：010–62772015, zhiliang@tup.tsinghua.edu.cn
印 装 者：天津鑫丰华印务有限公司
经　　销：全国新华书店
开　　本：185mm×260mm　　印　张：14　　字　数：304 千字
版　　次：2021 年 9 月第 1 版　　印　次：2025 年 1 月第 4 次印刷
定　　价：59.00 元

产品编号：091942–01

前言

2017 年，为贯彻落实国务院发布的《统筹推进世界一流大学和一流学科建设总体方案》，教育部等部门出台了《统筹推进世界一流大学和一流学科建设实施办法（暂行）》，旨在提升我国高等教育的综合实力和国际竞争力，最终实现"高等教育强国"的战略发展目标。这意味着我国未来的科技人才必须融入国际学术圈，拥有本学科领域的国际话语权。一流科技人才的标准之一就是能用英语直接阅读本学科的国际期刊文献，了解本领域世界前沿发展和研究的情况，用英语在国际学术研讨会和国际期刊上进行有效交流（蔡基刚，2018）。为此，越来越多的高校在公共英语课程体系中开设了学术英语类课程，以期为学生的专业学习和科研创新插上语言的翅膀。

本教材正是基于昆明理工大学 8 年来开设学术英语课程的教学实践而编写的，以项目学习为主线，践行语言知识技能与理工专业内容深度融合的理念，旨在培养学生对理工学科学术语篇的理解与产出能力，帮助学生熟练掌握英语文献检索方法，引导学生知晓学术讲座及学术会议的规范流程，启发学生在分析综合理工学科知识的同时，学会提出问题、进行批判性思考，并能用英语讲好中国科技故事。

本教材共分 7 个单元，包括学术英语阅读、学术英语写作、学术英语听力、学术英语交流、学术英语词汇、学术英语语法及科技英语翻译。每个单元围绕主题，将专业知识内容和听、说、读、写、译技能有机结合，有效融入互动练习，强化应用，并提供了拓展性资源，助力学生个性化学习。

立足互联网 + 背景，本教材与"理工学术英语"慕课有机结合（该慕课在学堂在线和中国大学慕课网开放），在单元结构方面构建了课前、课中和课后的混合式教学设计。具体安排如下：

一、**课前任务（Pre-class tasks）**

（1）慕课资源学习（Suggested MOOC resources）

（2）课前学习检测（Pre-quizzes）

二、**课中任务（In-class tasks）**

（1）主题概览（General glimpse of unit topic）

（2）知识点（Key points of unit topic）

（3）课内练习（In-class exercises）

（4）课中活动（In-class activities）

三、课后任务（After-class tasks）

（1）巩固性测试（Consolidating quizzes）

（2）思维导图（Mindmap）

（3）小组项目任务（Project task）

四、课外拓展资源（Extended resources）

在课前任务板块，要求学生提前学习慕课资源，并完成课前学习检测，以便教师在进行学情判断、开展课中任务教学时，能自主选择适合学生水平的教学知识点。课中任务板块设计了课中活动，旨在通过多元互动方式提高学生的参与度，并通过活动培养学生小组协作和沟通互评的能力；课内练习部分主要是对课中核心知识点进行强化。在课后任务板块，教材通过不同形式的练习帮助学生巩固单元知识点，并以思维导图的方式复习回顾单元所学要点，最后以小组活动方式完成项目任务。

值得一提的是，课后任务板块的巩固性测试中都设计了批判性思考任务，该部分将单元知识内容进行深化，有效融入课程思政元素，引导学生基于单元要点，结合现实深入思考，实现课程育人目标；同时，本教材还设计了小组项目任务，该任务基于真实的国际学术研讨会会议环节进行设计，并进行子任务拆分，在每个单元项目任务中进行实践，环环相扣，为学生参加学术研讨会奠定坚实的语言基础。

本教材融知识、能力和育人目标于一体，强调"在做中学"，建议教师在使用本教材时结合配套慕课课程，基于智慧教学采用混合式教学模式，鼓励学生多参与、多实践、多合作、多交流。

由于编者水平有限，教材中难免存在不足，敬请广大读者批评指正。

编者

2021 年 7 月

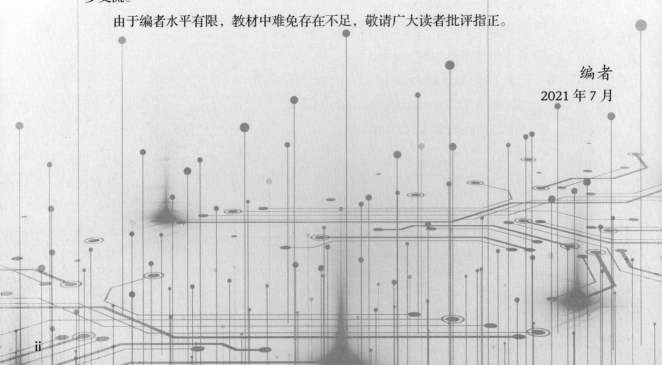

Contents

Unit 1
Academic Reading

Throughout your university study, you'll be responsible for completing different types of assessments: pre-quizzes, essays, group projects, tests, exams, etc. Teachers assign these in order to mark your learning progress. In order to prepare for these assessments, you should study effectively.

During this process, reading comes first. When you get to university, you'll find you need to get through a lot of readings from your reading list to prepare for an assignment. These may include academic papers, or chapters in edited books or textbooks. Many of these academic texts will seem quite difficult, especially academic papers. Have you ever tried to explore the characteristics of its language or structure?

Generally speaking, an academic paper will well present a systematic way of getting data, discovering new facts, developing new theories or reaffirming the previous work and solving new or existing problems, which makes its structure unique and various because of differences in disciplines. There are also commonly acknowledged prestigious journals in different fields. Do you have a basic understanding of the top journals in your field? You can start your reading journey from the pre-class tasks.

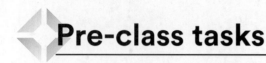
Pre-class tasks

❶ Suggested MOOC resources

You can scan the QR code to get a general idea of variations in structure of an academic paper in different fields.

- Overview of academic papers on geoscience
- Overview of academic papers on civil engineering
- Overview of academic papers on electrical engineering
- Overview of academic papers on metallurgical engineering
- Overview of intensive reading of academic papers on chemistry

❷ Pre-quizzes

1. What is the most commonly used structure in academic papers?

   A. RMID.   B. IMRD.   C. IRDM.   D. ILMRD.

2. Which of the following methods is NOT involved in research on civil engineering?

   A. Theoretical method.   B. Experimental method.

   C. Instrumental method.   D. Numerical method.

3. Generally speaking, how many types of papers are there in the electrical engineering field?

   A. Four.   B. Three.   C. Five.   D. Two.

4. Which of the following statements is NOT true about the grammatical features of academic papers?

   A. There are a lot of declarative sentences for the scientific facts.

   B. There are many long and difficult sentences for discussion on authors' viewpoints.

   C. There are numerous active voices for objectivity.

   D. There are lots of nonfinite verbs making analyses more scientific and precise, such as gerund and prepositional phrases.

5. What information can we NOT infer from the title "Increasing Stability and Activity of Core-shell Catalysts by Preferential Segregation of Oxide on Edges and Vertexes: Oxygen Reduction on Ti-Au@Pt/C"?

A. Research method.   B. Research goal.

C. Research question.   D. Research target.

In-class tasks

General glimpse of academic reading

Academic reading is the most essential step for academic learning. As a college student, you may be assigned numerous reading tasks on various topics, from impacts of the greenhouse effect on global warming to countermeasures for natural disasters like volcanic catastrophe during your academic learning, which are more challenging compared with those tasks in general reading. In addition, academic reading materials are mostly of various types and unique features.

1.1.1 Different types of academic reading materials

Depending on your subject, you may be reading journal articles, reports, case studies and books. Generally speaking, what you read extensively or intensively during your academic journey can be called as scientific literature, which comprises scholarly publications that report original, empirical or theoretical work in natural and social sciences, and within an academic field.

1.1.2 Classification based on the form

Scientific literature can be classified into the following types based on its form: journals, monographs, conference proceedings, graduation papers or dissertations; technical reports, science news, patents, product specifications, governmental publications and standards, etc.

Here we choose three types to illustrate in detail.

1.1.2.1 Journals

A scientific journal is a periodical publication intended to further the progress of science, usually by reporting new research. The research article is one of its types. The research article usually:

- Gives a full report on new research conducted by the authors;
- Contains abstract, introduction, methods, results, discussion, and conclusion;
- Gives detail for others to evaluate the findings or repeat the experiment;
- Cites other researches.

And the letter/note is another type, which:

- Reports a significant research result that does not require an extensive study;
- Is a brief article, typically within 2–4 pages;
- Is not divided into sections;
- Has citations within.

The third type is review article, which usually:

- Reviews several previously published works on one topic;
- Reports on work done by many scientists;
- Has citations within.

1.1.2.2 Conference proceedings

Conference proceedings usually reveal the latest discoveries, results, achievements, and developing tendencies in the field concerned. They are reports of presentations made at professional meetings and may be the whole articles or just abstracts of the presentations.

1.1.2.3 Patents

A patent is an exclusive right granted for protecting an invention, which describes a new invention and provides legal rights for the inventor.

1.1.3 Classification based on the processing depth of the research sources

Scientific literature can also be divided into the following three types based on the processing depth of the research sources.

1.1.3.1 Primary literature

In the field of sciences, the primary literature presents the immediate results of research activities. It often includes analyses of data collected in the field or laboratory, and presents original research and/or new scientific discoveries.

Here are some examples: original research published in peer-reviewed journals, dissertations, technical reports, and conference proceedings.

1.1.3.2 Secondary literature

The secondary literature summarizes and synthesizes primary literature, and it is usually broader and less current than primary literature. It includes literature review articles and books. Most information sources in the secondary literature contain extensive bibliographies, and they can be useful for finding more information on a topic.

1.1.3.3 Tertiary literature

The tertiary literature presents summaries or condensed versions of materials, usually with reference to primary or secondary sources. They are a good place to look up facts or get a general overview of a subject. Textbooks, dictionaries, encyclopedias and handbooks are typical examples.

1.1.4 Features of academic reading

1.1.4.1 More new or technical words

Many textbooks and journal articles are written in formal academic language, and subject-specific jargon will be used too. The following is an example—one paragraph of an academic paper from *Applied Nanoscience* that you will not fully understand unless you already know or can deduce what the terms refer to:

> Diesel particulate filter (DPF) is an advanced technology adopted in diesel vehicles to control particulate matter emissions. However, particulates get accumulated in the DPF and have to be regenerated periodically to reduce the backpressure. In the present work, Ceria, which is an excellent catalyst, has been coated over the DPF as nanofibers to ensure passive regeneration at a lower temperature, which aids in the continuous regeneration without soot accumulation. The cerium oxide nanofibers were synthesized by hydrothermal synthesis and characterized. The ceria nanofibers were coated on FeCrAl alloy by dip-coating method, and the regeneration studies

were done by thermogravimetric analysis (TGA) and CO_2 emission analysis. (Gautham et al., 2020)

At the beginning of the semester, you will have to learn the terms each new paper introduces. Help yourself by identifying words new to you and assimilating them fully into your vocabulary. In particular, learn what certain terms mean, which does require time and effort. For example, the paragraph cited above includes terms that are related to vehicle and transportation, such as "diesel particulate filter", "emissions", "backpressure", "nanofibers", "soot", and "regeneration". It may also include more specific terms such as "catalyst", "cerium oxide", "dip-coating", "thermogravimetric", "CO_2", and many other words that abound more in academic reading than everyday reading.

1.1.4.2 Complex sentences

Some textbooks or papers are definitely more user friendly. Titles, subtitles and margin notes all give helpful hints to the author's intentions, but even then, some complex sentences need to be carefully and deliberately deconstructed for the full message to be clear. For example:

The figure shows that the efficiency curves, corrected by considering the internal heat transfer contribution, are shifted toward the measured quasi-adiabatic curves, thus proving the reliability of the proposed experimental method for the heat transfer evaluation and the correction of the measured compressor efficiency map. (Gautham et al., 2020)

1.1.4.3 Dense paragraphs

In academic reading, it is common to read dense paragraphs that make it difficult to decipher the information. At this time, knowing how paragraphs are constructed can help a reader sort out the information and decide which points are the most important.

Now that we know how unique academic reading is, how can we start our academic reading effectively? Active learning and effective reading require more engagement than just reading the words on the page. In order to learn and retain what you read, it's a good idea to do things like circling key words, skimming and scanning, and reflecting on what you are learning.

Normally, we can gather information, gain knowledge and perform academic tasks through academic reading. All these tasks require not only simple comprehension, but also a full understanding of the basic structure of academic papers and good command of reading strategies, which help you to summarize, synthesize, and critically analyze the papers.

1.2
Basic structure of academic papers

Readers in various fields ranging from mechanical engineering to chemistry will expect the same basic structure from technical reports and papers. After examining thousands of different papers, people have identified four main sections that many technical papers have in common: introduction, methods, results, and discussion. Together, these four sections are known as IMRD (See the figure below). By following a general IMRD structure, you can ensure that your audience can find the information they're looking for.

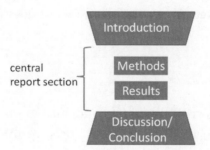

The conventional academic papers always follow the layout of IMRD, however, there are some variations among different disciplines. Sometimes academic papers on biological medicine usually follow the IRDM layout, but papers on electrical engineering include introduction, theoretical principles, simulation, and results (Scan the QR code to learn the two different layouts).

Let's review these four sections in detail.

1.2.1 Introduction

The introduction section states the problem or the question(s) you intend to address through research. It typically includes the following parts:

- Statement of the topic you are about to address;
- Current state of the field of understanding (Often, we call this a literature review);
- Problem or gap (What do we need to know? What still needs to be understood in the field? What has been left out of previous research? Is this a new issue that needs some directions?);
- Plan to solve the problem (Forecast statement that explains, very briefly, what the rest of the paper will entail, including a possible quick explanation of the type of research that needs to be conducted).

1.2.2 Methods

Regardless of what you did for your research, the methods section needs to be very clear, specific, detailed, and only focused on research itself. It typically includes the following parts:

- Set of procedures followed and approaches adopted by the researcher (How does the researcher proceed to collect the data?);
- Experimental materials or equipment (What does the researcher use to collect the data?).

1.2.3 Results

The results section is critical for your audience to understand what the research showed. Use this section to show tables, charts, graphs, quotes, etc., from your research. It typically includes the following parts:

- Findings of the study based on data collected from the methods section;
- Comparisons with what was expected or with results from other studies.

1.2.4 Discussion

The discussion section mainly focuses on authors' interpretations and opinions of the results, which serves as a bridge between current study and the previous related ones. It typically includes the following parts:

- Discussion of the key results and explanations of them;
- The limitations of your study;
- Implications and future study.

1.3

Skills for academic paper reading

Academic reading can be kind of difficult. But it may also be easy for you to find out the major points of an academic paper, because all academic papers ought to follow some fairly strict conventions in their structures. If you realize that academic papers are written in a particular style, you will understand what the author is saying. Only when you figure out the author's arguments can you make comments on the text, the content, the way the information is presented, and draw conclusions about the usefulness of the paper in general or more specifically to your research or your course. There are some basic skills to help you read dense, lengthy academic papers efficiently and effectively.

1.3.1 Consider the paper as a whole

Consider the paper as a whole. You need to determine something about the purpose, the audience and the content of the paper before you start reading. Look for clues in the title and/or subtitle, the acknowledgement (if any), the author affiliation or address, the first footnote or endnote, and the author's biographical note.

Here are some questions to guide you in considering the paper as a whole:

- Who is writing the paper? (Getting clues from the name, credentials, and affiliations)

- What are the author's qualifications? (Getting indications from information such as university or research affiliation or company)

- To whom is the author addressing? (Getting hints from the publication or journal itself and the first couple of paragraphs)

- What is the paper about? (Getting ideas from the abstract or conclusion sometimes)

1.3.2 Skim strategically to identify the main purpose and argument in the text

Before you read the text from beginning to end, skim it strategically to locate the author's main purpose and argument. Having the author's purpose and main argument in mind can help you read and interpret the rest of the text. These are sections where you are likely to find information about the author's purpose and argument:

Abstract: The abstract is an "executive summary" that appears in academic texts, usually as a paragraph at the top. As you read the abstract, try to identify the text's purpose, the main problem it deals with or question it answers, its main findings, and why readers should care. Abstracts are densely written—do not despair if you must re-read them. It is worth researching the terms in the abstract if you do not understand them.

Introduction: This is a real gem. The introduction of an academic paper often provides clear statements about the author's purpose, the question it answers, and its main points.

Conclusion: Pay close attention here, even if you assume the conclusion might be repetitive. The author may re-phrase a key point in a way that makes it clearer to you. This may also be the only place in the paper where the author discusses unanswered questions. These questions can help prepare you for discussion or fuel a written reflection.

1.3.3　Skim for the organization or "architecture" of the paper

Before you read the text from beginning to end, skim it to get a sense of its organization or "architecture". Doing this gives you a mental map that helps you see the different parts of the paper and its function in the overall argument. This perspective can help you read and process the text more easily. Strategies for building a mental map of the article's organization include:

Introduction (again): Look for a "forecasting statement" in the introduction. In addition to telling you about the author's purpose and argument, the introduction often provides one or more statements that preview the content and structure of the paper. Such statements give you a road map that helps you interpret the rest of the paper.

Section headings: Flip through the paper to read through all the section headings. Doing so can help you see the overall structure of a paper.

As you read the body of the text, use your knowledge about the main point of the paper and context clues from your discipline as you decide which parts of the paper deserve most of your energy, and where you can skim.

1.3.4　Read the paper and pay attention to its writing

As you read, watch for what the author is saying and how it is said, which requires that you read the paper to understand how the author presents the evidence and makes it fit into the argument. At this time, you should also take the time to look up any unfamiliar terms. There are many standard ways to keep the author's argument separate from the evidence, like "for example", "as Professor Source said", or "in my study area, I found that...". Also, you can look for transition words and phrases (like "however", "despite", "in addition", etc.) and the various word clues authors leave when they switch from their voice to that of their sources.

1.3.5 Pay attention to visual information

Images in textbooks or journals usually contain valuable information to help you grasp a topic more deeply. Graphs and charts, for instance, help show the relationship between different kinds of information or data, for example, how birth rate changes over time, how a virus spreads, etc.

Data-rich graphics can take longer to "read" than the text around them because they present a lot of information in a condensed form. Give yourself plenty of time to study these items, as they often provide new and lasting insights that are easy to recall later.

In brief, academic reading is a social activity. When you are reading, engage with your professor and peers, discuss your questions, and help your friends out. Always keep in mind that reading academic writings is like you're participating in a conversation with the authors.

1.4
Abstract reading

1.4.1 In-depth reading

Directions: *Read the following abstract of a paper carefully and identify what elements are mainly included in the abstract.*

①We investigated the influence of English proficiency on ERPs elicited by lexical-semantic violations in English sentences, in both native English speakers and native Spanish speakers who learned English in adulthood. ②All participants were administered a standardized test of English proficiency, and data were analyzed using linear mixed-effects (LME) modeling. ③Relative to native learners, late learners showed reduced amplitude and delayed onset of the N400 component associated with reading semantic violations. ④As well, the N400 late learners showed reduced anterior negative scalp potentials and increased posterior potentials. ⑤In both native and late learners, N400 amplitudes to semantically appropriate words were larger for people with lower English proficiency. ⑥N400 amplitudes to semantic violations, however, were not influenced by proficiency. ⑦Although both N400 onset latency and the late ERP effects differed between L1 and L2 learners, neither correlated with proficiency. ⑧Different approaches to dealing with the high degree of correlation between proficiency and native/late learner group status are discussed in the context of LME modeling. ⑨The results thus indicate that proficiency can modulate ERP effects in both L1 and L2 learners, and for some measures (in this case, N400 amplitude), L1–L2 differences may be entirely accounted for by proficiency. ⑩On the other hand, not all effects of L2 learning can be attributed to proficiency. ⑪Rather, the differences in N400 onset and the post-N400 violation effects appear to reflect fundamental differences in L1–L2 processing. (Newman et al., 2012)

An abstract is a self-contained, short but informative paragraph that describes what an academic paper is mainly about. Generally speaking, the purposes of writing an abstract are selection and indexing, which can provide readers with useful information to help them determine whether it is worthwhile to read the whole paper. Meanwhile, an abstract will always increase the chances of retrieving the paper in databases because it includes key terms.

Generally speaking, elements included in an abstract are as follows:

- Topic/Literature/Knowledge gap;
- Primary research objectives;
- Methods employed in solving the problems;
- Important findings or results obtained;
- Implications or value of the study

Based on the analysis above, we can identify that sentence ① mainly puts forward the primary research objective, and sentence ② tells us methods employed in solving the problem. In sentences ③–⑧, important findings or results obtained are shown, while sentences ⑨ and ⑪ present major implications or value of the study.

For further understanding of the elements included in an abstract, an in-class exercise is given.

In-class exercise:

Directions: *Read the following abstract carefully and identify the elements included in the abstract. Then write down the corresponding numbers of sentences in the following table.*

①Wildfires have a significant adverse impact on air quality in the United States (U.S.). ②To understand the potential health impacts of wildfire smoke, many epidemiology studies rely on concentrations of fine particulate matter (PM) as a smoke tracer. ③However, there are many gas-phase hazardous air pollutants (HAPs) identified by the Environmental Protection Agency (EPA) that are also present in wildfire smoke plumes. ④Using observations from the Western Wildfire Experiment for Cloud Chemistry, Aerosol Absorption, and Nitrogen (WE-CAN), a 2018 aircraft-based field campaign that measured HAPs and PM in western U.S. wildfire smoke plumes, we identify the relationships between HAPs and associated health risks, PM, and smoke age. ⑤We find the ratios between acute, chronic noncancer, and chronic cancer HAPs health risk and PM in smoke decrease as a function of smoke age by up to 72% from fresh (<1 day of aging) to old (>3 days of aging) smoke. ⑥We show that acrolein, formaldehyde, benzene, and hydrogen cyanide are the dominant contributors to gas-phase HAPs risk in smoke plumes. ⑦Finally, we use ratios of HAPs to PM along with annual average smoke-specific PM to estimate current and potential future smoke HAPs risks. (O'Dell et al., 2020)

Sentence(s)	Elements
	Topic/Literature/Knowledge gap/Primary research objectives
	Methods employed in solving the problems
	Important findings or results obtained
	Implications or value of the study

1.4.2 Jigsaw reading

Directions: *Read the following sentences with different numbers. Then put the sentences into the correct order to form the abstract of the paper entitled "Influence of Genetically Modified Soya on the Birth-weight and Survival of Rat Pups".*

(1) A group of female rats were fed GM soya flour before mating and pregnancy.

(2) The control group of females were fed traditional soya and the third group of females, the positive control group, received feed without any soya.

(3) The study showed that there was a very high rate of pup mortality (55.6%) in the GM soya group in comparison with the control group and the positive control group (9% and 6.8% respectively).

(4) Moreover, death in the first group continued during lactation, and the weights of the survivors are lower than those from the other two groups.

(5) Investigations of the influence of GM soya on the birth rate and survival of the offsprings of Wistar rats were performed.

(6) It was revealed in these experiments that GM soya could have a negative influence on the offsprings of Wistar rats.

(7) The weight and the mortality rate of the newborn pups were analyzed.

1.4.3 Visual interpretation

Directions: *Explain the underlying relationship between the following graphical abstract and summary selected from the paper entitled "Human Stem Cell-Derived Neurons Repair Circuits and Restore Neural Function".*

Graphical Abstract:

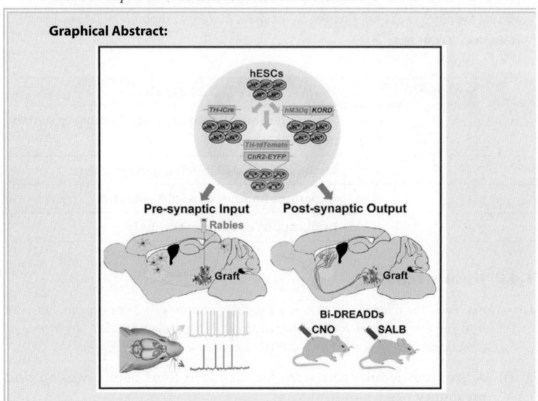

Summary: Although cell transplantation can rescue motor defects in Parkinson's disease (PD) models, whether and how grafts functionally repair damaged neural circuitry in the adult brain is unknown. We transplanted hESC-derived midbrain dopamine (mDA) or cortical glutamate neurons into the substantia nigra or striatum of a mouse PD model and found extensive graft integration with host circuitry. Axonal pathfinding toward the dorsal striatum was determined by the identity of the grafted neurons, and anatomical presynaptic inputs were largely dependent on graft location, whereas inhibitory versus excitatory input was dictated by the identity of grafted neurons. hESC-derived mDA neurons display A9 characteristics and restore the functionality of the reconstructed nigrostriatal circuit to mediate improvements in motor function. These results indicate similarity in cell-type-specific pre- and post-synaptic integration between transplant-reconstructed circuit and endogenous neural networks, highlighting the capacity of hPSC-derived neuron subtypes for specific circuit repair and functional restoration in the adult brain. (Xiong et al., 2020)

1.5
Text reading

The Cup-in-hand Walk

1   Have you ever done the cup-in-hand walk and spilled your drink? It's a common event. The Krechetnikov Fluid Physics Lab at the University of California in Santa Barbara usually doesn't focus on this type of problem, but after seeing enough people doing the cup-in-hand walk and spilling, they decided to look into it. The research focused on cylindrical shaped cups used commonly to hold coffee, tea, or hot cocoa. The problem involves complex motions but is solvable.

Some physics

2   Pendulums are commonly discussed in physics classes. Historically they were used to keep time. The most popular pendulum is a swing. Sit on a swing and give it a push and it goes back and forth. Because the swing is connected to a fixed point with string or chain, it moves along a circular path. The initial push moves the swing in the direction of the push, and the tension in the string pulls the swing upward. Then Earth's gravity pulls the swing downward. This process

continues until the initial energy imparted to the swing is dissipated to the environment. However, if you continually push the swing by pumping your legs, then you keep it in motion, and if you make sure you pump your legs at just the right time, then you can make the swing go higher. Swinging by pumping your legs is an example of what scientists call a driven oscillator.

3   When you walk, even though you may only be going in one direction along the floor, there is still a back and forth, or oscillatory, motion to your walk. Walking in and of itself is a complicated motion. The body rotates slightly along the head-to-foot axis, moves a bit up and down with each step, and arms tend to move about the joints (shoulder, elbow, and wrist). When you walk with a cup full of fluid in your hand, your walking motion changes a bit. For example, there is less rotation about all of the arm joints. Some of the motion energy of walking gets transferred to the cup and to the fluid in the cup. Try it out!

4   Think back to the swing. If you pump your legs at the wrong time, the swing does not get any higher. If you pump them at just the right time (dependent on where the swing is located), you go higher. It turns out that the coffee cup has similar features. If you input energy at just the right time, you can make the liquid in the cup go higher. It turns out that the combination of the cup dimensions and common walking makes for just the right combination to get spills.

The research

5   How do you get data for such an event? Take a video! Then process the time frames to get the time and location of the coffee and person, as well as the velocities, and accelerations. The researchers had people walk naturally with an average speed between 0.5 and 2.5 meters per second while either focusing on the cup or not focusing on the cup. The researchers focused on taking measurements of the vertical motion of the cup and the motion of the cup parallel to the floor.

6   The cup was rigged such that light would turn on whenever the fluid in it reached the rim. The circuit consisted of a lead (a sensor) connected to the rim of the cup, an LED that lit up when the circuit was closed, and a conducting fluid in the cup, which closed the circuit when it reached the rim. The conducting fluid was just coffee mixed with salt.

7   After analyzing their data, they found that all directions show an oscillatory type of motion in the cup, however, not all contribute in the same way to a spill event. The researchers considered the natural frequencies of oscillation for the cylindrical cup under ideal situations (no friction, incompressible fluid, no swirling), which are well known from studies pertaining to things like rocket fuel canisters. The dimensions of coffee cups usually have a radius of 2.5 cm and a height of 5.7 cm to a radius of 6.7 cm and a height of 8.9 cm. The most common cup studied had a radius of 3.5 cm and a height of 10 cm. Remember that the dimensions of the cup are like the parameters of a swing. You pump your legs during swinging at just the right time, which is determined by the length of the swing and where you are in your swinging motion. If the liquid is to increase in amplitude in the cup, then the cup must be "pumped" by the walking movements at just the right time, which is determined by the cup's dimensions.

8   What they found is that the initial back-and-forth motion from walking forward affects the initial sloshing or displacement of liquid along the side of the cup. The side-to-side or lateral motion of walking affects the liquid oscillations when the motion is close to the natural oscillations that are allowed by the cup dimensions, but these are not as close to the forward-back motions of stepping. The vertical motions do not contribute significantly to the natural oscillations of the liquid in the cup. Surprisingly, the natural oscillations of forwarding stepping motion coincide well with the natural oscillations allowed for common cup dimensions. What does this mean? That walking tends to "pump" the back and forth motion of the liquid in the cup at just the right time so that it increases in height along the cup's side. Eventually, it reaches the rim and spills. This result implies we need some new cup designs, or perhaps we shouldn't walk around with our cups!

9   The research also noted that most coffee spilling occurs within the first 7 to 10 steps (4 to 5 meters) of walking, and occurs earlier when people quickly reach their regular walking speed (their initial acceleration). The initial acceleration causes the initial displacement of liquid in the cup. The bigger the initial acceleration, the bigger the initial displacement of the fluid in the cup.

10   It turns out that the more focused you are on the cup and spilling, the less likely you are to spill. These subjects reached their regular walking speeds more

slowly, the initial displacement of liquid was less, and they required more steps before the height of the liquid along the side of the cup increased to the rim. Also, you can alter your movement if you see the fluid nearing the rim.

Future research and applications

11 This research suggests a few things. The first two may seem obvious: Don't fill a cup too much if you walk with it. If you are walking with a cup of liquid, focus on it and adjust your motion if you see it is about to spill. The less obvious suggestions deal with improvements on cup designs that would reduce the resonant oscillations. Suggestions on cup design improvements include: flexible coffee cups, a series of ringed ridges along the inside of the cup, or broken ridged rings along the inside of the cup. All these cup design suggestions would dissipate the energy of the oscillations so the fluid would not reach the rim and spill.

1.5.1 Problem-based exploration

Directions: *Work in groups to discuss the following pictures. After discussion, each group needs to present the common, underlying principle on physics. You are encouraged to refer to the following questions during the process of discussion.*

- Can you walk holding a cup of coffee without spilling it? Why?
- Can you relate a swing to the cup-in-hand walk? How?
- Do you have any solutions to prevent the water in the cup from spilling?

1.5.2 Academic reading circle

1. Complete the following text structure exercise based on your understanding.

Text structure		
Parts	Paragraphs	Main idea
Part one	Para(s) _____	
Part two	Para(s) _____	
Part three	Para(s) _____	
Part four	Para(s) _____	

2. List out transition words and phrases in the text that help you grasp its structure.

_____

_____

_____

_____

3. Paraphrase the following sentences.

(1) The circuit consisted of a lead (a sensor) connected to the rim of the cup, an LED that lit up when the circuit was closed, and a conducting fluid in the cup, which closed the circuit when it reached the rim.

_____

_____

(2) You pump your legs during swinging at just the right time, which is determined by the length of the swing and where you are in your swinging motion.

_____

_____

4. Visualize the descriptions in Paragraph 6 in your own way.

5. Make a PowerPoint presentation to illustrate how this text fits into the IMRD structure.

After-class tasks

❶ Consolidating quizzes

1. **Read the following text and choose the correct answers to the questions that follow.**

Boredom has, paradoxically, become quite interesting to academics lately. In early May, London's Boring Conference celebrated seven years of delighting in the dullness. At this event, people flocked to talks about the weather, traffic jams and vending machine sounds among other sleep-inducing topics. What, exactly, is everybody studying? One widely accepted definition of boredom is "the distasteful experience of wanting, but being unable to engage in satisfying activity".

But how can you quantify a person's boredom level and compare it with someone else's? In 1986, psychologists introduced the Boredom Proneness Scale, designed to measure an individual's overall tendency to feel bored. By contrast, the Multi-dimensional State Boredom scale, developed in 2008, measures a person's feelings of boredom in a given situation.

Boredom has been linked to behavior issues, including inattentive driving, mindless snacking, excessive drinking, and addictive gambling. In fact, many of us would choose pain over boredom.

One team of psychologists discovered that two-thirds of men and a quarter of women would rather self-administer electric shocks than sitting alone with their thoughts for 15 minutes.

When researching this phenomenon, another team asked volunteers to watch boring, sad, or neutral films, during which they could self-administer electric shocks. The bored volunteers shocked themselves more and harder than the sad or neutral ones did.

But boredom isn't all bad. By encouraging self-reflection and daydreaming, it can spur activity. An early study gave participants abundant time to complete problem-solving and word-association exercises. Once all the obvious answers were exhausted, participants gave more and more incentive answers to combat boredom: A British study took these findings one step further, asking subjects to complete a creative challenge (coming up with a list of alternative uses for a household item). One group of subjects did a boring activity first, while the others went straight to the creative task. Those whose boredom pumps had been primed were more productive.

In our always-connected world, boredom may be a hard-to-define state, but it is fertile. Watch paint dry or water boil, or at least put away our smartphone for a while, and you might unlock your next big idea.

(1) When are people likely to experience boredom, according to an accepted psychological definition?
    A. When they don't have the chance to do what they want.
    B. When they don't enjoy the materials they are studying.
    C. When they experience something unpleasant.
    D. When they engage in some routine activities.

(2) What does the author say boredom can lead to?
    A. Determination.
    B. Mental deterioration.
    C. Concentration.
    D. Harmful conduct.

(3) What is the finding of one team of psychologists in their experiment?
    A. Volunteers prefer watching a boring movie to sitting alone deliberating.
    B. Many volunteers choose to hurt themselves rather than endure boredom.
    C. Male volunteers are more immune to the effects of boredom than females.
    D. Many volunteers are unable to resist boredom longer than fifteen minutes.

(4) Why does the author say boredom isn't all bad?
    A. It stimulates memorization.
    B. It may promote creative thinking.
    C. It allows time for relaxation.
    D. It may facilitate independent learning.

(5) What does the author suggest one do when faced with a challenging problem?
    A. Stop idling and think big.
    B. Unlock one's smartphone.
    C. Look around oneself for stimulation.
    D. Allow oneself some time to be bored.

2. **Scan the QR code and read the three academic papers given to see how their structures are laid out.**

3. **Critical thinking:** It is said that it is not advisable for all soldiers in an army to march across one bridge at the same time. Is it true? Why or why not? What can we get from this?

(Points for references: phenomenon of resonance; pros and cons of physics in daily life; the same is true for human being; how to get along with other people friendly and harmoniously)

❶ Mindmap

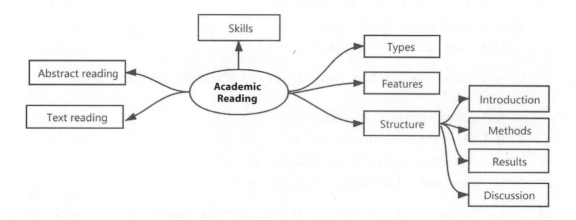

Ⅲ　Project task

Suppose you plan to participate in an international conference for college students, and are expected to submit your research report and make a presentation. Please check the details of the conference below and fulfill the task.

The 7th International Conference for College Students

Theme of the conference: Sustainability and Innovation: HEED (Human, Environment, Economy, and Development of Technology)

Sub-topics of the conference:

- Human Existence and Sustainability;

- Environment, Sustainability, and Innovation;

- Economic Development: Sustainability and Innovation;

- Technology, Sustainability, and Innovation.

Ⅳ　Extended resources

1. **TED talk given by Helen Czerski: "The Fascinating Physics of Everyday Life"**

Brief information: Physics doesn't just happen in a fancy lab—it happens when you push a piece of buttered toast off the table or drop a couple of raisins in a fizzy drink or watch a coffee spill dry. Become a more interesting dinner guest as physicist Helen Czerski presents various concepts in physics that you can become familiar with using everyday things found in your kitchen.

2. **Further paper reading: "A Study on the Coffee Spilling Phenomenon in the Low Impulse Regime"**

Brief information: When a glass of wine is oscillated horizontally at 4 Hz, the liquid surface oscillates calmly. But when the same amount of liquid is contained in a cylindrical mug and oscillated under the same conditions, the liquid starts to oscillate aggressively against the container walls and results in significant spillage. This is a manifestation of the same principles that also cause coffee spillage when we walk. In this study, we experimentally investigate the cup motion and liquid oscillation during locomotion. The frequency spectrum of each motion reveals that the second harmonic mode of the hand motion corresponds to the resonance frequency of the first anti-symmetric mode of coffee oscillation, resulting in maximum spillage. By

applying these experimental findings, a number of methods to suppress resonance are presented. Then, we construct two mechanical models to rationalize our experimental findings and gain further insight; both models successfully predict actual hand behaviors.

Unit 2

Academic Writing

Many people would say that writing is the hardest task to fulfill. Sometimes it is even an impossible task to fulfill. Hardly had we thought about why we need to write. Is it for the grade we need? Is it for the job or promotion? Absolutely not. It's more than that. As a psychologist says, "You need to learn to think, because thinking makes you act effectively in the world."(Scan the QR code for more information)

Writing is a way to cultivate our thinking. If we want to write, we have to think hard and differently to produce something interesting and readable. Needless to say, it's hard to start writing. Many of us take it for granted that we are not good at writing. Ask yourselves if you have done any writing work. Tell yourselves that you don't have to be good at writing for you are not to be writers. Writing is a way to help you think logically and orderly. Through writing, you can view your weakness in thinking patterns and the need to read more to accumulate you knowledge.

Writing is a way to relieve. Many people have felt the intense stress from work and life. When you take your pen or dance on your keyboard, your consciousness will bring you to the magic world you create and you can find and explore the beauty of the world. Writing in this sense is a means of controlling your mind and a process to create a world of your own.

Writing is also a way to communicate your ideas. Whatever you have written, you are in communication with others at the moment you finish writing. You write in different forms to arouse others' resonance, empathy or reflection. You write on observations, on evidence, on facts or sometimes on your emotions.

As a college student, you are advised to write down your ideas or gains on what you have learned in summarized paragraphs to demonstrate your digestion of the knowledge, and then convert your developed ideas into an article or paper. Some of you may say, "If I cannot write a logical summary, how can I write in an academic way to communicate with others?" This is what this unit will talk about. In this unit, a guideline of how to put your ideas into written words will be given. You will learn how to write the introduction of a paper, and some tips for writing the results. How to write an abstract and a title will surely be talked about, too. Let's start the thrilling journey from the following tasks.

Pre-class tasks

❶ Suggested MOOC resources

You can scan the QR code to learn how to get yourself prepared for writing an academic paper.

- Literature search in academic writing
- Framework of academic paper and introduction sections
- Citation, plagiarism, MLA and APA
- Revising, editing and submitting

❷ Pre-quizzes

1. In which section should you put your experimental data?

A. The introduction section. B. The methods section.

C. The results section. D. The discussion section.

2. How can you construct a purpose statement?

A. Topic + reasons + key terms.

B. Topic + theory + results.

C. Purpose noun + action verb + topic.

D. Key words + definition + findings.

3. What do you usually discuss in the discussion section? (*There may be more than one correct answer.*)

A. Commenting on the data.

B. Interpreting the results.

C. Pointing out limitations and implications.

D. Summarizing findings.

E. Calling for further research.

F. Explaining detailed research process.

4. Which of the following statements is NOT true about a title?

A. A good title is accurate and concise.

B. A good title is eye-catching.

C. A good title summarizes the central idea of a paper.

D. A good title cannot be a sentence.

5. Which of the following statements is NOT true about an abstract?

A. A good abstract is brief and informative.

B. A good abstract is objective.

C. A good abstract must also follow the IMRD format.

D. A good abstract is often 3% to 5% of the length of the paper.

In-class tasks

2.1

General glimpse of academic writing

Writing and publishing academic papers in English is a challenge for most students. However, it has gradually become a part of higher education and career development. In this unit, we will focus on academic writing and how to write each part of a paper will also be discussed.

Generally speaking, an academic paper is a formal piece of writing in which academics present their views and research findings on a chosen topic. The purpose is to advance knowledge in a research field with evidence, to explain new ideas and make them accessible to others, or to solve practical problems.

2.1.1 Features of academic writing

Academic writing is a particular style of expression, which is quite different from the conversational, casual style. It's also different from the writings in newspapers or novels. It has its unique features: formality, objectivity, accuracy and complexity.

For example, when you are writing "it would be convinced that…" instead of "I think…" in your paper, it becomes more objective. Or it is advisable to use citations to express your views, for example, "Paul (2019) argues that…", which will tell your readers that you are doing a formal research. To make your point specific and accurate, you can replace phrases with single words; for example, you can use "a group of art students participate in the show" to substitute "Art students participate…"

2.1.2 Steps of academic writing

Different genres of academic writing follow similar steps. There are usually six steps of writing a research paper. First, we need to select a topic. The second step is to collect and evaluate data. After the preparation of data, draw up an outline. An outline is a guide to writing, giving us a clear picture of the relationship among ideas in the paper. Based on the outline, we may produce the first draft of the paper. Although the title and abstract always appear at the beginning of the paper, they should be written after the entire paper is done so as to cover all the necessary information regarding the research. The last step is to revise and edit the paper.

2.2
Selecting a topic

Among the six steps, the first step—topic selection is of great importance. A good beginning is half done, so is a research paper. However, topic selection has become a major obstacle for many students to start their writing. Then how to choose a topic? Let's look at the following four steps of selecting a topic.

2.2.1 Steps of selecting a topic

We start by choosing a research topic that interests us and brainstorming ideas that come into our minds with regard to our research. Firstly, we need to read extensively to see what would be the fun topic we want to devote to. Then we narrow our topic to a focus. Meanwhile, we may consult our professors or an expert to get constructive suggestions. Thirdly, we should read books and academic journals and ask ourselves questions after reading a book or a paper, such as:

- Is there a way to expand upon the existing research?
- Is there a way to approach the research from a different perspective?
- Is there a way to apply the same techniques to a different subject?

In academic writing, originality is crucial, but it is hard to be totally original. We may combine the pre-existing elements of the research in an original way or try to take existing research further.

Fourthly, we need to attend academic conferences and academic lectures. Those conferences and lectures may inform us of the latest academic development and provide us with inspiration about the topic.

2.2.2 Criteria for selecting a topic

A good topic must meet certain criteria. We should consider the topic from the following perspectives.

A good topic is valuable. It should be of research value, of interest to other scholars in the field, and meet the needs of certain communities. A good topic is scientific, which means that scientific methods are applied in conducting research. Also a good topic is original because originality is the soul of scientific research. And a good topic should be feasible. When choosing a topic, we need to take certain things into consideration, such as our professional interests, our previous experiences of research, and conditions for the research.

In-class exercise 1:

Directions: *Number the following steps which describe the process of choosing a topic to put them in the appropriate order.*

☐ Decide how practical it is to work on this topic.

☐ Find something in your subject area that you are interested in.

☐ Summarize your idea in one sentence.

☐ Decide how much you already know about the topic.

☐ Talk about your ideas.

☐ Think about a possible working title.

☐ Look for sources.

☐ Make a plan.

2.2.3 Ways to narrow down a topic

Actually a research beginner usually selects a too broad topic. To avoid the problem, we can first select a general topic and then narrow it down to a smaller and workable one. There are four ways to narrow down a topic. First, analyze different components of the topic and pick one of them. Second, make use of the SOCR model (S stands for Similarities; O for Opposites; C for Contrasts; R for Relationships). Third, ask several smaller questions about the broad topic. Fourth, analyze the topic in terms of certain simple, straightforward questions like who, when, what, where, why and how.

For example, we are interested in the distribution of natural Korean pines. Subject the topic to the smaller questions: Where can we conduct the research? And how can we do the research? Then we get a better topic: "distribution of natural Korean pines in Baihe Forestry Bureau based on spatial models". It is better than topics like "distribution of natural Korean pines in Baihe Forestry Bureau" or "distribution of natural Korean pines based on spatial models".

In-class exercise 2:

Directions: *Narrow down the following topics to more practical research topics.*

(1) Physics: _____

(2) Writing: _____

(3) Drama: _____

(4) Biology: _____

2.3
Writing a title

The title and the abstract are like a hat on a head or the front door to a house, and they give a powerful first impression. Generally speaking, many readers will decide whether to read the entire paper or not just based on its title and abstract. As the first readers, publishers of journals may also determine a rejection or acceptance of the paper by reading the title and abstract. So what can be counted as a good title?

2.3.1 Standards for a good title

A good title is clear, concise, accurate, and eye-catching. It summarizes the central idea of the paper concisely and accurately. Meanwhile, it is interesting enough to attract readers' attention. Look at the following examples:

- An Examination of the Impact of Online Professional Development on Teacher Practice
- The Calculation of Small Molecular Interactions by the Differences of Separate Total Energies—Some Procedures with Reduced Error
- Using Ontology for Integrated Geographic Information System

2.3.2 Structure of a title

The structure of the title must follow certain grammatical patterns. In many research fields, the most commonly used grammatical structure pattern is noun phrases, for example, "Application of Organic Petrology in the Brake Industry". However, compounding title with two or three parts has become increasingly popular.

Look at the title: "Study on the Suppression of Aeroelastic Instability of 2-D Wing by Nonlinear Energy Sinks".

How can we modify the title into a better one? We can delete "study on" from the title. Although it is common to use phrases like "study on / research on / analysis of / investigation of" in Chinese titles, it is viewed as redundancy in English titles. Therefore, for the title above, we could change it like this: "The Suppression of Aeroelastic Instability of 2-D Wing by Nonlinear Energy Sinks".

2.3.3 Tips on writing a title

To write a suitable title for a research paper, there are some tips. First, condense the paper's content in a few words. Second, place key words in the forward position in a title, which is a good way to capture readers' attention. Third, use appropriate descriptive words. A good title should contain important information in the research paper and define the nature of the study. Fourth, avoid lesser-known abbreviations and jargon.

2.4
Writing an abstract

An abstract is an overview of a research paper. When we read a paper, we will focus on the abstract to decide whether we want to read the whole paper because the abstract is the simplest statement on the content of an article.

2.4.1 Elements of an abstract

Abstracts in various fields are written in a similar way. A well-written abstract must be brief, informative, and objective. It usually contains five elements. Here is a table that shows the typical order of the five elements in an abstract.

Table 2-1 Elements of an abstract

Elements	Necessary*/optional
Background (importance of the topic, reference to the current literature / identification of a knowledge gap)	
Purpose(s) of the present research	*
Methods used	
Results/findings	*
Conclusions/implications / value of the current study	

We may call it BPMRC. An abstract should include B—research background, P—purpose(s) of the present research, M—methods used, R—results/findings, and C—conclusions/implications/value of the current study. Of all the elements, those two with*, namely the purposes and the results, should always be included in an abstract.

In-class exercise 3:

Directions: *Complete these statements about an abstract to check your understanding of what an abstract is.*

(1) An abstract is _____.

(2) Abstracts are very useful because _____

_____

_____ .

(3) The three typical features of abstracts are _____

_____

_____ .

2.4.2 Steps of writing an abstract

The abstract is located at the beginning of a paper. However, it is always written when we finish the whole paper. The abstract functions as the summary of our paper. We may not have a clear and integrated idea of what will be concluded unless the paper is done, so it is not advisable to write the abstract before finishing the paper.

There are two typical types of abstracts, namely descriptive abstract and informative abstract. A descriptive abstract tells the readers what information the paper mainly contains, outlines the purpose, methods, scope of the paper, and introduces the subject. An informative abstract contains specific information from the paper, including the purpose, methods, scope of the paper, the results, conclusions, and recommendations. Let's walk through an example to see the different parts of an abstract.

Recently, layered copper chalcogenides Cu_2X family (X=S, Se, Te) has attracted tremendous research interests due to their high thermoelectric (TE) performance, which is partly due to the superionic behavior of mobile Cu ions, making these compounds "phonon liquids". **(Background)** Here, we systematically investigate the electronic structure and its temperature evolution of the less studied single crystal $Cu_{2-x}Te$ by the combination of angle resolved photoemission spectroscopy (ARPES) and scanning tunneling microscope/spectroscopy (STM/STS) experiments. **(Methods)** While the band structure of the $Cu_{2-x}Te$ shows agreement with the calculations, we clearly observe a 2×2 surface reconstruction from both our low temperature ARPES and STM/STS experiments which survives up to room temperature. Interestingly, our low temperature STM experiments further reveal multiple types of reconstruction patterns, which suggests the origin of the surface reconstruction being the distributed deficiency of liquid like Cu ions. **(Results)** Our findings reveal the electronic structure and impurity level of Cu_2Te, which provides knowledge about its thermoelectric properties from the electronic degree of freedom. **(Conclusion/significance)** (Liu et al., 2021)

In the example above, background comes first, followed by methods, results and conclusion. Although you have finished your abstract in this order, your writing is not done yet. The last step for you to write your abstract is to count how many words are there in your abstract, because an abstract should be as brief as possible. Usually, it is 3% to 5% of the length of the paper. For a paper or a report, it is usually around 200 words. And in this section, present tense, past tense, and present perfect tense are often adopted.

Table 2-2   Number of sentences in each element of an abstract

Elements of an abstract	Number of sentences
Background	one sentence
Purpose(s)	one topic sentence, and supporting sentences if necessary
Methods	two or more sentences to give specific information
Results	one sentence, or more if necessary
Conclusions and significance	one or two sentences

One more example is provided for you to check the steps of writing an abstract. By locating the elements one by one, you can also count the number of sentences in each element to avoid writing too long.

Although a large body of literature has examined the effect of social capital on health and theoretical models suggest a reciprocal relationship between the two variables, there are relatively few studies that have investigated the effect of mental health on social capital. **(Background)** This paper evaluates the impact of mental health on the stock of social capital using data from the cross-sectional 2012 (N = 21,844) and 2002 (N = 31,089) Canadian Community Health Survey—Mental Health editions. **(Purpose)** Mental health was measured retrospectively as self-rated mental health, past year mental health conditions, and past 30-day psychological distress. Given the reciprocal relationship, we used an instrumental variable approach with family history of mental health problems as the instrument and examined forms of social capital—sense of belonging and workplace social support—that are largely measures of social capital provided by non-family members in the community and workplace. **(Methods)** The analysis suggests there are large and significant associations between measures of mental health and both outcomes, which persist in the instrumental variable analyses. **(Results)** These findings highlight the urgent need for policy makers to implement greater prevention and treatment of poor mental health, and provide greater support for individuals with poor mental health so they can build and maintain their social capital. **(Conclusion/significance)** (Lebenbaum et al., 2021)

2.4.3 Sentence patterns for writing an abstract

In abstract writing, certain sentence patterns are often employed, which may help you, especially beginners, to present your research findings more idiomatically.

2.4.3.1 For background information

To highlight the importance of a topic:

- Recently, there has been renewed interest in…

To identify a knowledge gap of the previous research:

- For the past three decades, studies of X have been restricted to…

2.4.3.2 For research purpose(s)

- The present study aimed to explore the relationship between…
- In this study, techniques for X were developed and applied to…

2.4.3.3 For research methods

- The research is based on four case studies.
- A combined qualitative and quantitative methodological approach was used to…

2.4.3.4 For results

- This study identifies…
- The experimental data suggested that…

2.4.3.5 For conclusions or significance of the study

- These findings provide a solid evidence base for…
- The findings can contribute to a better understanding of…

2.4.4 Abstract breakdown activity

Directions: *Study the following abstract, and then identify the functions of the numbered sentences based on Table 2-1.*

①Management consultancy has been developing for more than 100 years. ②It originated in the United States, before spreading to other countries. ③Localization plays an important role in the expansion of management consultancies. ④This, according to Crucini (1999), is the process of "adapting and translating management tools and ideas to work in a foreign market with a different economic or social background". ⑤The history of the spread of management consultancies is first described, followed by an outline of the localization processes of foreign management consultancy firms in Italy and China. ⑥Some common problems encountered in the processes are then identified. ⑦Finally, advice is given on how to achieve successful localization.

2.5
Writing an introduction

An introduction has a clear function as the first part of your paper. It sets the tone for the reader by giving some ideas of the content. Generally speaking, an introduction is composed of the topic, background, previous studies or literature review, and the purpose of the study.

Table 2-3   Elements of an introduction

Elements	Necessary*/optional
Topic	*
Definition and key terms	
Background	*
Previous studies (literature review)	*
Purpose	*
Theory	
Justification/reasons for your research	
Organization/outline of your structure	

2.5.1 Steps of writing an introduction

We have a clear picture of what could be included in the introduction section. But how should we organize it? We can start with the Three Moves method:

- **Move 1:** Introduce and review previous research;
- **Move 2:** Indicate a gap in the previous research;
- **Move 3:** State the purposes and significance of the present research.

To better understand these moves, let's see an example. Read the following introduction section of a paper on soil remediation and find out the types of information the author has included in this section.

①With the rapid development of the chemical industry, heavy metals in environment increase rapidly and go beyond the normal range, which has seriously polluted the soil. ②Such soil contamination leads to deterioration of environmental quality and does harm to humans' health. ③So, it is important to control soil pollution caused by heavy metals.

④Phytoremediation is considered to be a cheap and safe repair technique for it uses plants to absorb heavy metal pollutants in soil and transports metals to the air for storage. ⑤In the past 20 years, phytoremediation has drawn much attention. ⑥Much research has been done on herbs belonging to hyperaccumulator, but the results are not satisfactory because of small biomass, underdeveloped root, short growth cycle and other factors. ⑦Woody plants can overcome the shortcomings of herbs, but the studies on them are quite few.

⑧This research investigated six woody plants, aiming at finding out some species that can be widely used in phytoremediation to deal with heavy metals in soil. ⑨The study will provide a new approach to soil remediation. (Purakayastha & Chhonkar, 2009)

2.5.2 Sentence patterns for writing an introduction

The following are some sentence patterns that could be used in the Three Moves method.

Move 1

- The role of X in Y has received increased attention across a number of disciplines in recent years.
- Results from earlier studies demonstrate a strong and consistent association between...
- The causes of X have been the subject of intense debate within the scientific community.
- X has been attracting considerable interest since it was discovered in...
- X has been the subject of many classic studies in...
- There is a growing body of literature that recognizes the importance of...
- The last decades have seen a growing trend towards...
- Recent developments in the field of X have led to a renewed interest in...
- The past thirty years have seen increasingly rapid advances in the field of...
- In the last few decades, there has been a surge of interest in the effects of...
- X proved an important literary genre in the early Y community.
- A key issue is the safe disposal of...
- It is now well established that X can impair...
- Data from several studies have shown that...
- Previous research has established that...
- Recent studies have reported that...
- It is well established from a variety of studies that...
- Surveys such as that conducted by Smith (1998) have shown that...

Move 2

- X and its consequences are important but understudied causes for concern.

- No previous study has given sufficient consideration to...

- However, up to now, far too little attention has been paid to...

- This indicates a need to understand the various perceptions of X that exist among...

- Most studies in the field of X have only focused on...

- The research to date has tended to focus on X rather than Y.

- Paul's analysis does not take account of..., nor does he examine...

- Most studies of X have only been carried out in a small number of areas.

- Research on the subject has been mostly restricted to limited comparison of...

- However, few writers have been able to do any systematic research into...

Move 3

- This prospective study was designed to investigate the use of...

- In this paper, I attempt to defend the view that...

- This paper has four key aims. Firstly...

- The central thesis of this paper is that...

- The specific objective of this study was to...

- An objective of this study was to investigate...

- This research examines the emerging role of X in the context of...

- This study systematically reviews the data for..., aiming to provide...

- The main aim of this study is to investigate the differences between X and Y.

- There are two primary aims of this study: (a) to investigate...; (b) to ascertain...

- This study seeks to obtain data which will help to address these research gaps.

- This study sought to answer the following specific research questions...

- This study provides new insights into...

- This study sheds light on...

- The originality and importance of this study is that it explores...

2.5.3 Matching activity

Directions: *Read the introduction part of a paper and use the Three Moves method to find sentences that belong to the different moves. Find out the indicators or patterns that show the functions of these sentences.*

Thermoelectric (TE) materials play a vital role in the pursuit of green and renewable energy because it can realize direct conversion of waste heat to electric energy. The TE performance of a material is evaluated by the dimensionless figure of merit (zT), defined as $S2\ \sigma T/\kappa$, where S is the Seebeck coefficient, σ is electrical conductivity, T is the temperature, and κ is thermal conductivity coefficient. The search for TE materials with high zT value has become the central issue for the development of thermoelectric technology. The zT value can be enhanced by tuning the electron and phonon transports to achieve high electrical conductivity and low lattice thermal conductivity. Following such strategy, many types of TE materials have been synthesized and explored, greatly enhancing zT over the past decades.

Recently, copper chalcogenides compounds Cu_2X (X = S, Se, Te) have attracted lots of attention for their exceptionally low thermal conductivity and high TE performances. The achieved zT is as high as 1.5 in $Cu_{2-x}Se$, 1.7 in $Cu_{2-x}S$, and 1.1 in $Cu_{2-x}Te$ at 1,000 K, which are among the top values in bulk TE materials. Comparing to Cu_2S/Se, Cu_2Te is expected to have lower thermal conductivity due to heavier tellurium atoms and larger carrier mobility due to the less electronegativity and less ionic bond strength, making Cu_2Te an important TE material candidate.

It is believed that the superionic diffusion of Cu ions, which suppresses the lattice thermal conductivity, plays an essential role in the high TE performance of Cu_2X materials. While the detailed structure and liquid like behavior of Cu ions have been carefully studied in Cu_2Se, the investigation on the electronic properties of Cu_2Te is essentially lacking up to date, although the Cu ions are expected to be more mobile in Cu_2Te due to the weaker ionic bonds. The previous studies on Cu_2Te revealed a complicated phase diagram as a function of temperature with at least five different crystalline phases above room temperature (up to 900 K). Yet the low temperature phase of Cu_2Te remains unexplored.

More importantly, the electronic degree of freedom also plays an important role in the TE performance of materials. For example, in our recent angle resolved photoemission spectroscopy (ARPES) study on Cu_2Se, we observed the band reconstruction across the α-β structural phase transition, leading to the enhancement of the Seebeck coefficient near 400 K. However, the electronic structure of Cu_2Te and its temperature evolution remains nearly unexplored, despite several calculation results.

These motivations inspire us to investigate the structural and electronic properties of Cu_2Te at low temperature. X-ray diffraction (XRD) measurement confirms the lattice structure without structural transition from 100 K to room temperature. By performing ARPES measurement, we directly observe not only the complete band structure of Cu_2Te which shows agreement with the calculation results, but also the folded band at the $\bar{M}$ point up to room temperature, which strongly evidences the 2×2 surface reconstruction. These findings are further confirmed by our scanning tunneling microscope (STM) surface topographic measurements. Moreover, our STM measurement reveals multiple surface reconstruction patterns in addition to the 2×2 surface reconstruction. We speculate the large amount of Cu deficiencies that are uniformly distributed due to the liquid-like behavior of Cu ions leads to the ubiquitous surface reconstruction. Our result provides important information on the structural and electronic properties of $Cu_{2-x}Te$, which provides knowledge about its TE properties from the electronic structure aspect. (Liu et al., 2021)

2.6
Writing methods and results

In this part, you will get a clear picture of the experiment. And the following questions should be answered: How were the topics chosen? What tools were used? Where and in what condition was the experiment conducted? How did you design your study, and what steps did you follow when the data were collected? Which criteria were used for selecting subjects? How was the questionnaire designed and administered? How were the samples or respondents chosen? How was the interview conducted? How were the statistics analyzed? When all the questions are answered, we can better understand the methods section.

2.6.1 Features of methods

Generally speaking, the methods section is just an objective presentation of the methods and procedures of the experiment. The features are as follows:

- All the steps of the experiment are presented in this part.
- It's a straightforward report of procedures and materials.

- No problems, matters of discussion or rationales are mentioned in this part.

The following two samples are extracts from two papers. Read through each of them to learn how the author describes the methods to the readers. (The underlined parts show how the author describes the method part.)

High-quality $Cu_{2-x}Te$ single crystals <u>were grown using</u> the solid phase reaction. **(General description)** Cu (99.9%), Te (99.999%) powders <u>in a mortar ratio of 2 : 1 were mixed</u> using a mortar for 30 min and <u>placed into</u> an alumina crucible. The crucible <u>was sealed in a quartz ampoule under vacuum</u> and subsequently heated to 850 ℃ in 10 h. <u>After reaction</u> at this temperature for 400 h, the ampoule <u>was cooled to</u> 300 ℃ in 100 h and cooled to room temperature in air. $Cu_{2-x}Te$ single crystals with black shiny metallic luster were obtained. **(Procedures of the experiment)**

Both ARPES and STM measurements <u>were carried out in</u> ultrahigh vacuum (UHV) environment. **(Experimental condition)** Fresh and clean surfaces of $Cu_{2-x}Te$ were obtained by *in situ* cleavage along (001) plane. ARPES experiments <u>were performed at beamline</u> 5-2 in Stanford Synchrotron Radiation Lightsource (SSRL), U.S.A., beamline I05 in Diamond Light Source (DLS), U.K., beamline APE in Elettra synchrotron, Italy and lab-based ARPES system in Tsinghua University, China. **(Experimental locations)** Experimental data <u>were collected</u> by Scienta R4000 analyzer at SSRL and DLS, DA30 analyzer at Elettra and Tsinghua University. **(How experimental data are collected)** The total convolved energy and angle resolution were better than 20 meV and 0.2°, respectively. In STM/STS experiments, cleaved samples were transferred to a cryogenic stage kept at 77 K and 5.2 K for STM/STS experiments. PtIr tips were used for both imaging and tunneling spectroscopy measurements which were all calibrated on the surface of silver islands grown on p-type Si (111)-7×7. Lock-in technique <u>was employed</u> to obtain dI/dV curves with an extra 5 mV modulation at 997.233 Hz alongside the normal DC sample biases. **(Techniques employed)** In addition, the method of theoretical calculation is described in Appendix A. (Liu et al., 2021)

This study <u>included a secondary analysis of</u> Statistics Canada's cross sectional 2012 Canadian Community Health Survey—Mental Health (CCHS-MH), which <u>sampled individuals aged 15 years and older from the 10 provinces</u> (Statistics Canada, 2013). **(Participants)** <u>Excluded from the survey's sampling frame</u> were individuals living on indigenous reserves or settlements, homeless individuals, full-time members of the Canadian armed forces, and those living in prisons or long-term care institutions

(Statistics Canada, 2013). The <u>overall response rate</u> was 68.9% (Statistics Canada, 2013). **(Questionnaire validity)**

Of an initial sample of 25,113 respondents, 21,844 and 11,373 were included in the main analysis sample for <u>sense of belonging and workplace social support</u>, respectively. **(Conditions)** Individuals with missing data were excluded from the analysis. Of the individuals who were dropped in the sense of belonging analyses, 2024 were excluded as they were ages 15–19 and had not been asked the questions on child abuse. In addition to the exclusion of individuals aged 15–19, the workplace social support analyses also excluded 12,093 individuals who were not asked the required questions, which included respondents older than age 75, those who did not work in the past 12 months, or respondents without coworkers/supervisors. Missing data on primary independent and dependent variables was small (<1% for each variable). <u>Study variables were presented separately for individuals</u> with and without missing data in Table 1. <u>Mental health and social capital variables</u> were generally similar across both groups with greatest differences found for education and age, with individuals with missing data more likely being older and less educated. **(Variables)** (Lebenbaum et al., 2021)

2.6.2 Elements of results

All the results and findings in the experiments should be stated in a concise and well-organized manner, which means the results section shouldn't be too long. Another feature is that there is no repetition of details mentioned in the methods section.

In other words, there should be an overview of the experiment or a summary of the findings. And also, there should be detailed presentation of the representative data, graphic aids, or their analysis. Along with these two, there's still another one. That's the detailed presentation of the findings. When writing the results, the following elements should be included:

- Stating the facts;
- Comparing and contrasting;
- Analyzing cause and effect;
- Illustrating with graphic aids.

For example, we can see the different elements of the results from the following two extracts.

It is indicated that the maximum burial and temperature for the shales occurred in the third burial and established the maximum thermal maturity before Yanshanian extensive uplift and erosion (Figures 8 and 10). **(Stating the facts)** The Qiongzhusi and Wufeng-Longmaxi shales were deeply buried during the early Mesozoic, and the burial depth had reached approximately 6,000 and <7000 m, respectively. Zhu et al. (2018) found that VRo showed an abrupt offset in the VRo-depth profile over the Middle/ Late Permian unconformity. The Well JY2 penetrated a basalt body with a thickness of 70 m at a depth of 2,340–2,410 m recorded by well completion reports. **(Comparing and contrasting)** Clearly, anomalously high or notable changes in Ro were measured in the Ro-depth profile (Figure 11). **(Illustrating with graphic aids)** This trend may suggest an increasing heat flow as a result of eruption of the Emeishan flood basalts (Zhu et al., 2016, 2018) in southwestern Sichuan Basin, which uncomfortably overlie the late-Middle Permian Maokou Formation (Xu et al., 2001). **(Analyzing cause and effect)** (Wang et al., 2021)

Cu_2Te has a hexagonal layered like crystal structure and its space group is $P6/mmm$ (no. 191). **(Stating the facts)** It is easily cleaved along the (001) plane to obtain a fully tellurium terminated surface, as shown in Figures 1(a) and 1(b). The schematic of Brillouin zone (BZ) and its projection to (001) surface are shown in Figure 1(c) with high symmetry points labeled. The photoemission core level spectrum of the cleaved sample is shown in Figure 1(d). The characteristic peaks of Cu $3p$ and Te $4d$ electrons are clearly observed in the photoemission core level spectrum. The crystal structure of $Cu_{2-x}Te$ has been confirmed by the temperature dependent XRD measurements in Figure 1(e). **(Illustrating with graphic aids)** We do not observe any signature for structural transition from 100 K to room temperature. Large terraces with flat (001) surface and sharp step are obtained after cleavage, as shown in the large scale STM topographic image in Figure 1(f). The measured step height is about 0.73 nm, which is consistent with the lattice constant c, given by the line profile in Figure 1(g). **(Comparing and contrasting)** (Liu et al., 2021)

2.6.3 Sentence patterns for writing methods

2.6.3.1 Describing methods

- X-tests were used to analyze the relationship between…
- Both X and Y measurements were carried out to…

- In order to assess X, repeated measures ASPR were used to...
- Variables X and Y indicated that...
- Five individuals were excluded from the study on the basis of...
- Prior to undertaking the investigation, ethical clearance was obtained from...
- Further data collection is required to determine exactly how X affects Y.

2.6.3.2 Presenting data in a table or graph

- The most striking aspect of this graph is...
- In Figure 2, there is a clear trend of decreasing...
- What is interesting about the figures in this table is...
- This table is quite revealing in several ways. First, unlike the other tables...
- The differences between X and Y are highlighted in Table 2.
- Data from this table can be compared with the data in Table 3 which shows...
- As shown in Figure 1, the emission of industrial gas increased by 121%.
- According to the data obtained from the current study, flavonoid production increased remarkably as salinity levels increased.
- As can be seen from Table 1, London has the largest underground railway system.

2.6.3.3 Expressing positive or negative results

- This result is significant at...
- There is a significant correlation between...
- There was a significant difference in...
- No significant reduction in X was found compared with...
- There was no evidence that X was detected in...
- T-tests found no significant differences in mean scores on the X and Y subscales.
- No significant correlation was found between A scores and B scores.
- None of these differences between the two groups was evident.
- The more surprising correlation is related to...
- The correlation between X and Y is interesting because...
- Interestingly, there were also differences in the ratios of...

- X revealed/showed/demonstrated/illustrated/exhibited/presented…

- X exceeds/records…

- X ranges from…to…

- X is characterized by…

- Compared X with Y, X matches…

- X is similar to / consistent with…

2.6.4 Call-out activity

Directions: *Read the following four pictures, and then illustrate the functions of them based on the information you have got.*

EDS composition of our samples

Number of region	Atomic conc. of Cu (%)	Atomic conc. of Te (%)	Ratio Cu/Te
1	65.66	34.34	1.912
2	61.72	38.28	1.612
3	62.97	37.03	1.701
4	65.06	34.94	1.862
5	64.78	35.22	1.839
6	66.02	33.98	1.943
7	63.95	36.05	1.774
8	66.59	33.41	1.993
9	65.22	34.78	1.875
Average			1.823

Picture A

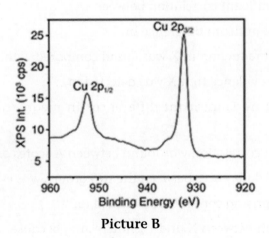

Picture B

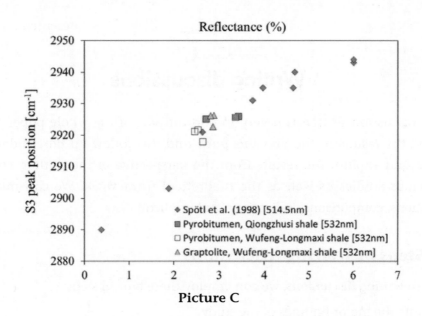

Picture C

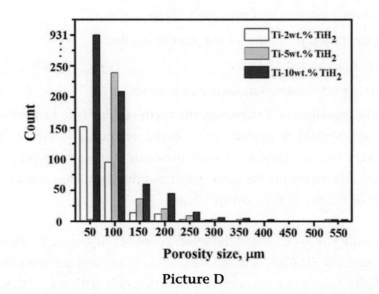

Picture D

Picture A: _____

Picture B: _____

Picture C: _____

Picture D: _____

2.7
Writing discussions

The discussion section is a very important part of the whole paper. We have presented the results in the previous part, and this follow-up part is designed to examine and explain the results from the perspective of the author, combining the previous studies as well as the theoretical framework. We can make some explanations, comparisons, indications and implications.

2.7.1 Steps of writing discussions

When writing discussions, we can employ these typical steps:

- State the major findings of the study;
- Explain the meaning and the cause of the findings;
- Relate the findings to those of the similar studies;
- Analyze unexpected findings;
- Suggest the implications in theory or practice.

Specifically speaking, in discussions, the methodology is to be mentioned again, and the methods should be justified. And then, we should interpret the results. It is also necessary to cite agreement with previous studies to make comparisons. And also make comments on the data, point out discrepancies, and call for further research. Now let's move to the example below.

①Prior work has documented the effectiveness of psychosocial intervention in improving quality of life (QoL) and reducing stress in patients suffering from various disorders. Epstein, for example, reports that orthopedic patients participating in a two-week multimedia intervention program improved across several QoL indices, including interpersonal conflict and mental health. ②However, these studies have either been short-term studies or have not focused on patients whose disorder was stress-related. ③In this study we tested the extent to which an extended three-month stress management program improved QoL among a group of patients being treated for stress-related skin disorders such as eczema.

④We found that in virtually all cases, participation in our three-month stress-management program was associated with substantial increases in the skills needed to improve QoL. ⑤These findings extend those of Kaliom, confirming that a longer, more intensive period of stress-management training tends to produce more effective skills than when those skills are input over a shorter period via information transfer media such as leaflets and presentations (Kaliom et al., 2003). ⑥In addition, the improvements noted in our study were unrelated to age, gender or ethnic background. ⑦This study therefore indicates that the benefits gained from stress-management intervention may address QoL needs across a wide range of patients. ⑧Most notably, this is the first study to our knowledge to investigate the effectiveness of extended psychosocial intervention in patients whose disorder is itself thought to be stress-related. ⑨Our results provide compelling evidence for long-term involvement with such patients and suggest that this approach appears to be effective in counteracting stress that may exacerbate the disorder. ⑩However, some limitations are worth noting. ⑪Although our hypotheses were supported statistically, the sample was not reassessed once the program was over. ⑫Future work should therefore include follow-up work designed to evaluate whether the skills are retained in the long term and also whether they continue to be used to improve QoL. (Glasman-Deal, 2010)

The following is a simple analysis of the discussion section described above.

In sentence ①, the author revisits previous research.

In sentence ②, the author revisits the introduction section to recall specific weakness in the methodology used in previous studies.

In sentence ③, the author revisits the methodology used in this study.

In sentence ④, the author revisits and summarizes the results.

In sentence ⑤, the author shows where and how the present work fits into the research "map" of this field.

In sentence ⑥, the author recalls an aspect of the results that represents a positive achievement or contribution of this study.

In sentence ⑦, the author focuses on the meaning and implications of the achievements in this study.

In sentence ⑧, the author notes that one of the achievements or contributions of this study is its novelty.

In sentence ⑨, the author refines the implications of the results, including possible applications.

In sentences ⑩ and ⑪, the author describes the limitations which should direct future research.

In sentence ⑫, the author suggests a specific area to be addressed in future work.

2.7.2 Sentence patterns for writing discussions

2.7.2.1 Interpretations

- The results of this study indicate/show/suggest/confirm that...
- Our findings suggest a possibility of...
- In this study, we found/identified that...
- This could explain why...
- Our data are consistent with...
- Our findings on...agree with those reported by...et al., who...
- Our data differ from...
- Unlike...et al., we observed that...

2.7.2.2 Implications

- An implication of this is the possibility that...
- These findings may help us to understand that...
- This finding, while preliminary, suggests that...
- This finding has important implications for developing...
- These studies thus offer a new strategy to treat...
- The major strength of this study was...
- Our studies establish the... / Our approach is special as it not only..., but also...
- In this study, we showed for the first time that...
- Our studies serve as a proof-of-concept that...
- Our findings provide additional support for... /add to the accumulating evidence that suggests... / support the premise that...
- Our findings may be useful in... / will allow us to take the next step in...
- Adaptations of this study to other...could result in...

2.7.2.3 Limitations

- The limitations of the study are clear...

- The findings of the study are restricted to...
- This study addressed only the question of...
- The lack of...means that we cannot be sure...

2.8
Revising and editing

When we finish the first draft of the paper, it is only half done. We need to revise and edit it. No matter how much time we spend on the first draft, we can always find a few mistakes to correct and some points to polish. Revising and editing enable us to evaluate our ideas, generate and test new ideas, and polish and improve the overall argumentation.

2.8.1 Revising

Generally, we start the revision by reading over the whole paper quite quickly. Circle any mistakes that you spot, but concentrate on the overall flow, that is, you should check the entire framework.

First, check whether the purpose of the paper is complete and logical or not. Second, ask yourself some questions about arguments: Is the viewpoint clear, and can it stand up to test? Are there any angles to the arguments that you've missed? Third, double check if the reasoning is thorough and logical. Fourth, go through the whole organization of the paper again to see if the entire framework is complete. Fifth, polish your language.

For language polishing, it involves the following aspects:

- Grammar: Is the verb tense correct? Does the verb agree with the subject?
- Sentence: Is the sentence structure correct and diverse?
- Vocabulary: Is the language varied and accurate? Are there any unnecessary or confusing words?
- Spelling and punctuation: Are spelling and punctuation correct?

2.8.2 Editing

Once we finish the revision of the entire framework, we start polishing paragraphs and sentences. You can follow the steps below:

- Check if there is unity in the paragraphs.
- Focus on topic sentences: Is there a topic sentence in each paragraph?
- Examine if it is necessary to add or delete some materials.
- Check the citation and documentation: Do citations and documentations follow the editorial style required in a certain academic discipline and the target journal to which you will submit your paper?

2.8.3 Final checklist

Before the submission of the paper, proofreading it is the final and essential step. We may check the following:

- Abstract;
- Originality;
- Theoretical framework;
- Methods;
- References.

We should get prepared to revise our paper for many times before it gets published.

2.9
Getting to be published

2.9.1 Steps to submit to an aiming journal

When finishing the manuscript, many writers would try to figure out where to publish it. A good start is to scan the journal titles to decide which journals might accept papers in our field. Then we may read the recent papers published in the journals, analyzing their characteristics to see if they currently will accept work of the kind we are to submit.

After selecting the right journal, we should prepare the manuscript according to the specific requirements of the journal, which include the criteria of paper acceptance, printing format, length of the paper, the style for setting the references. These rules can be found on the journal's website and the notices in the journal.

After everything is ready, we can submit our paper. Most publishers and journals have built their own homepages, and we are supposed to submit the electronic copy of our paper on the website. Or we may send our paper to the executive editor by email.

2.9.2 Response to the reviewer's suggestions

After our submission of the paper to a journal, we will receive feedback on suggestions from reviewers if the paper is considered valuable. How should we react to the feedback? First, we need to write back politely with one or two paragraphs, expressing our appreciation for what they have done. Second, we should respond to the reviewers' feedback one by one. Quote the feedback first, and illustrate what improvements we have made. The following is an example of how the author responds to the feedback.

Feedback from the reviewer: Introduction needs to be improved: Although the current work is sufficiently novel to warrant publication, I believe that the literature coverage in Introduction is not complete, and the objectives are not very clear. I suggest that the scope of Introduction be broadened, and the novelty specified in that context. One possibility is to consider adding a detailed discussion on planar (2-D) cellulose network composite. Additionally, the composite properties must be compared with existing literature, although the matrix may not be the same. There are several successful stories, primarily by groups led by Prof. Yano, Prof. Berglund, and Prof. Oksman, for example, (Appl. Phys. A: Mater. Sci. Process. 80 (2005) 155–159, Appl Phys Lett 89 (2006), Cellulose 15 (2008) 555–559, Composites Part A 63 (2014) 35–44, Composites Part A 58 (2014) 30–35, Compos. Sci. Technol. 117 (2015) 298–306, Compos. Sci. Technol. 155 (2018) 64–71).

The author's improvement: Good suggestion! We have also added the references mentioned above into the manuscript. In my view, the planar (2-D) cellulose network was mainly fabricated by self-assembly behavior of one dimension cellulose materials, nano-sized cellulose fibers, nano-sized cellulose whiskers, etc, which also could be recognized as nanocellulose template (Page 4, Line 11) that we had described in this article.

Third, write about what other improvements we have made, and explain the reasons. (See more examples by scanning the QR code.)

Fourth, if we disagree with the suggestion or feedback by the reviewer, we should explain politely why we stick to the statement. If our explanation isn't accepted, we should consider shifting our submission to another journal.

Academic writing is not an easy task, but it is a fantastic journey. It involves more than writing skills. It is a way of expression. We hope that you can get some insights into academic writing and develop your ability to communicate in an international setting.

After-class tasks

❶ Consolidating quizzes

1. Complete the summary about the definition of the topic below with words and expression from the box.

examples	terms	dictionary	interpretation
shared knowledge	comment	knowledge	

When writing about a topic, you must clarify your **(1)** _____ (explain clearly what you mean by any key words you use) so that the writer and the reader have the same **(2)** _____. If you are new to the subject, you will need to define the most basic terms so that you understand them properly. As you gain **(3)** _____ of the subject, and if you are writing for specialists, the meaning of certain key terms can be assumed as part of **(4)** _____. You can use formal definitions from a(n) **(5)** _____ or an expert in the field, expand a definition with explanations or **(6)** _____, or make a(n) **(7)** _____ about the definition.

2. **Identify the main problems in the following abstract and try to improve it.**

Abstract: With the deepening of globalization and interdependence, the gradual formation of the global system has put forward new security requirements. The first need is to maintain the basic living environment and the survival and sustainable development of the component units. At the same time, the United Nations Report on Human Development also identifies seven dimensions of "human security": economy, food, health, environment, individuals, communities and politics. The proposal of this concept indicates that the concept of security has changed from a narrow sense of security with the state as the main body to a comprehensive and inclusive security concept, which also represents the convert of focus from the state to the people-centered. Based on the survival of human beings, this paper will mainly use qualitative analysis for the environmental dimension and put forward suggestions for sustainable development at this level. Through this research, we can greatly improve the cognitive ability of human beings to their own living environment, attach importance to global sustainable development, and then maintain human survival. Sustainable development and human security share the same goal orientation, both of which take human welfare as the ultimate goal. Therefore, solving global environmental problems is an important step for human existence and the basis for the economic development of all countries.

3. **Rewrite the following sentences in more formal academic English.**

(1) Crime was increasing rapidly, and the police were becoming concerned.

(2) I observed 43 students of a third-grade class at Barksdale School for two weeks.

(3) Scientists have developed various remote sensing approaches to monitor insect impacts.

(4) This study looks into the relationship between tree density and fruit size.

(5) We analyzed the experiment and what we found made us realize that the technique is quite complex.

4. **Critical thinking: Academic integrity is the commitment to and demonstration of honest and moral behavior in an academic setting. This is most relevant at the university level as it relates to providing credit to other people when using their ideas. In simplest terms, it requires acknowledging the contributions of other people. How do you comment on correct citation in writing?**

(Points for references: an adequate or accurate reference list; plagiarism; ethical rules; learn to cultivate the spirit of academic integrity; social core values)

5. You may have already done some reading, researching and thinking in your subject area. Based on the research you have done, complete the following plan as far as possible.

What is your topic?	
Why have you chosen this topic?	
Key questions (What do you want to find out about this topic?)	
What is your focus and/or working title?	
Purpose of the paper	
Tentative title	

Ⅱ Mindmap

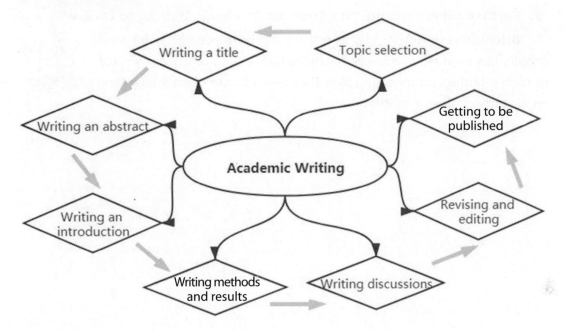

Ⅲ Project task

In this unit, you are supposed to specify these general topics chosen by your group members. You can ask questions to establish a focus for your topic. Then you can ask yourself some specific wh-questions to narrow down your topic.

- Intelligent buildings;
- Genetically modified (GM) food;
- Gas pollution;
- Future development in human health.

Ⅳ Extended resources

1. TED talk given by Margaret G. Stewart: "How YouTube Thinks About Copyright"

Brief information: Rights management is no longer simply a question of ownership; it's a complex web of relationships and a critical part of our cultural landscape. YouTube cares deeply about the rights of content owners, but in order to give them choices about what they can do with copies, mashups and more, we need

to first identify when copyrighted material is uploaded to our site.

2. Further paper reading: "It's Time for Academic Writing to Evolve"

Brief information: Academic articles can be impenetrable for most people, but even when readers do understand them, many are written in such a boring, unappealing way that they are not exactly engaging paper-turners. Does it matter?

Unit 3
Academic Listening

Many students find listening in English is one of the most difficult abilities to acquire, but this is an important part in our daily communication if we were abroad. Similarly, you need to get points from others before you share yours when you are in an academic meeting, a seminar, or a symposium. However, academic listening is different from daily talk in that the latter is casual and relaxing sometimes, while academic listening follows some patterns. The speaker in an academic lecture wants to make his points clear, logical and persuasive, so he would like to follow the same pattern in his written papers, with variations sometimes of course.

In this unit, with the help of listening examples, we hope you will understand basic structures of academic lectures, acquire skills for academic listening, such as taking notes while listening with a flow chart or summarizing main ideas with a mindmap. Now Let's start your academic listening journey.

Pre-class tasks

❶ Suggested MOOC resources

You can scan the QR code to get features and skills of academic listening.

- Structure of academic lectures
- Note-taking skills
- Key ideas in academic lectures
- Terminologies in academic lectures
- Digressions in academic lectures

❷ Pre-quizzes

1. **What is the feature of academic listening?**

A. Informative and well-structured.   B. Logical and complex.

C. Non-linguistic.   D. All of the above.

2. **Which of the following statements is true about the features of academic listening?**

A. The lecturer always presents a hypothesis or a theory when delivering a lecture.

B. The lecturer never follows the same structure of his academic paper when giving a lecture.

C. The lecturer always takes the IMRD structure when giving a lecture.

D. The lecturer may use various structures to organize his lecture.

3. **Which of the following methods is NOT involved in note-taking skills?**

A. Key sentences.   B. Mindmaps.   C. Symbols.   D. Abbreviations.

4. **Which of the following is NOT the way of presenting supporting details?**

A. A story.   B. A paraphrase.

C. An introductory phrase.   D. An academic reference.

5. **Which of the following techniques is NOT usually used to introduce a new concept?**

A. Examples.   B. Definitions.   C. Analysis.   D. Contrasts.

In-class tasks

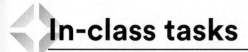

3.1

General glimpse of academic listening

Academic listening is an essential tool for academic communication. As a college student, you may take part in an academic meeting, a workshop, or a symposium, and it is quite necessary for you to get the main points of academic lectures from the speaker through listening. Therefore, it is important to enhance your ability of academic listening.

In the beginning, let's get a brief understanding of the purpose and features of academic listening.

3.1.1 Purpose of academic listening

Generally, we listen to the academic lectures to expand the scope of our knowledge, to keep up with the latest disciplinary knowledge, theories, equations and so on.

3.1.2 Features of academic listening

Lectures in academic listening are quite different from the conversational, daily casual talks. They are also different from political speeches, ministers' sermons, or even businessmen's sales presentations. Compared with other genres, academic lectures are distinguished as a prolonged and densely-informed monologue with typical discourse structures, so academic listening has its unique features: informative, well-structured, logical, challenging, as well as vivid.

3.1.2.1 Informative

In academic contexts, lecturers often inform, define, or explain the academic materials or clarify the points to the audience, so devices such as definition, classification, comparison and contrast, persuasion and evaluation are usually involved in the lectures. Actually, conveying information is regarded as the main purpose of academic lectures. The audience need to focus on information in lectures

and also complete information processing simultaneously while taking notes.

3.1.2.2 Well-structured

Recognizing the structure of a lecture may help you understand the main ideas that the lecturer is trying to communicate. It focuses on the following parts: outline, shifting to the next main point, introducing the supporting materials, and summarizing.

3.1.2.3 Logical

The academic lecture is a logical progression of materials, from general to specific, or from the parts to the whole, or from a problem to a solution.

3.1.2.4 Challenging

When listening to an academic lecture, some factors will influence your listening comprehension, such as pauses, hesitations, signaling cues or markers, emphasis, function words and digressions. All these may bring challenges to you in academic listening.

3.1.2.5 Vivid

It often refers to the appropriate use of visual aids in an academic lecture, including slides, handouts, whiteboard and ways of nonverbal communication.

3.2
Skills for academic listening

Academic lectures, including interactive lectures, professional meetings, posters and oral presentations, seminars, workshops and symposiums, are useful means of presenting information or delivering content to a large group of audience in an efficient way. Therefore, as college students, understanding academic lectures through listening is a necessity when participating in academic activities.

A lot of skills are involved in academic listening. This unit will cover the following aspects of listening skills: preparation and prediction, structure, note-taking, introductions, key ideas, terminologies, and digressions. After learning and practicing, we hope you can identify the purpose and scope of a lecture, distinguish relationships among units within the discourse, and deduce meanings of words from contexts.

3.2.1 Preparation and prediction

Many students are fearful of listening, and can be disheartened when they listen to something but feel they understand very little. To listen to an academic lecture effectively, you can do a lot of work before listening. The following are some tips:

- Find out the topic of the lecture to be delivered;
- Research the topic by reading the related sources or the assigned readings;
- Sort out subject-specific words and terms the lecturer may use;
- Check the meanings and pronunciations of the terms and words;
- Familiarize yourself with the subject and list out questions if possible;
- Bring loose-leaf papers or spiral-bound notebooks, or bring a laptop if necessary.

For example, if you are going to listen to a lecture about global warming, do your homework first. Read the related academic papers and search sources in the library, and pay more attention to some terms such as "CO_2", "greenhouse" and "deforestation". Then write down the questions, for example, "What factors affect global temperature?"

Prediction is a basic skill in listening comprehension. Its major objective is to enable the listener to listen with a clear purpose. Our knowledge of the world helps us anticipate the kind of information we are likely to hear. Moreover, when we predict the topic of a talk, all the related vocabulary stored in our brain is "activated" to help us better understand what we're listening to. As for the content, prediction mainly covers such areas as the general idea of the listening material, the questions that might be raised after listening, and the best answers to the questions among the choices given.

There are many good methods of predicting. The usual practice is to make a clever guess. However, predicting is not the same as guessing, since the listener has some kind of expectation by making use of the written information, his knowledge about the English language, his background knowledge about the topic being discussed, his general knowledge or experiences gained in life, and the method of logical argumentation.

In-class exercise 1:

Directions: *Predict the answers to questions (1)–(3). Then listen to the audio and choose the best answers to questions (4)–(6).*

(1) What species live in well-organized colonies?

(2) What species may live with human at home?

(3) What species does the audio refer to according to the given items?

(4) A. They help farmers keep diseases in check.
 B. Many species remain unknown to scientists.
 C. Only a few species cause trouble to humans.
 D. They live in incredibly well-organized colonies.

(5) A. They are larger than many other species.
 B. They can cause damage to people's homes.
 C. They can survive a long time without water.
 D. They like to form colonies in electrical units.

(6) A. Deny them access to any food.
 B. Keep doors and windows shut.
 C. Destroy their colonies close by.
 D. Refrain from eating sugary food.

3.2.2 The structure of academic lectures

In the previous two units, we have learned about the common structure of an academic paper. However, the lecturer may have various lecture structures to deliver the speech efficiently and logically. The following are some common lecture structures:

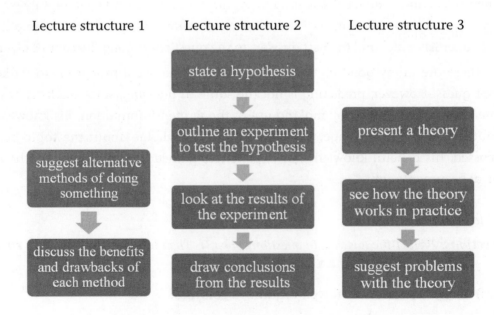

Lecture structure 1   Lecture structure 2   Lecture structure 3

Lecture structure 1:
- suggest alternative methods of doing something
- discuss the benefits and drawbacks of each method

Lecture structure 2:
- state a hypothesis
- outline an experiment to test the hypothesis
- look at the results of the experiment
- draw conclusions from the results

Lecture structure 3:
- present a theory
- see how the theory works in practice
- suggest problems with the theory

The structures of lectures are various according to the different studies and the speaker's way of delivering. As you listen to a lecture and take notes, an easy way to record a lecture structure is using line spacing to separate thoughts, ideas, etc. List the general points along the margin of the page. Leave some blank space below each point so that it will be easy to locate these main ideas when you review your notes after the lecture. You can also use the space to add details or explanations later on. Then indent as you list out more specific ideas and examples. Continue to indent each time the lecture moves from general points to specific ones. By using the space and indent, you can present the lecture structure clearly. For example:

> The first general point
> > A specific point related to the first general point
> > A second specific point related to the first general point
> > > A detail related to the second specific point (an example, a statistic, etc.)
> The second general point
> > (etc.)

In-class exercise 2:

Step 1: **Message-passing**

Directions: *Five students are assigned to one group, including four runners and one writer, who are required to stand at a distance between each other.*

- First, the teacher shows the first message on the paper to the first runner of different groups.

- Then, the first runner passes the message to the second runner in their group respectively.

- Then the message is passed on to the third and fourth runner in the same way.

- Finally, the writer takes down the message.

- The first group with a complete and correct message wins.

The messages are as follows:

(1) What's the perfect way to dunk a biscuit with your cup of tea?

(2) Holding the biscuit in a horizontal position has a significant effect on the amount of time that a biscuit can stay in hot liquid before falling apart.

(3) The answer is related to diffusion, in other words, the length of dunking time, and another factor is the temperature of the tea.

(4) The researchers have come up with an idea for a biscuit-holding device to make dunking biscuits easier.

Step 2: Information-filling

Directions: *Review the messages your group has taken down, and think about its structure. Then listen to the audio* "The Science of Dunking" *and fill in the blanks below.*

The structure of "The Science of Dunking"

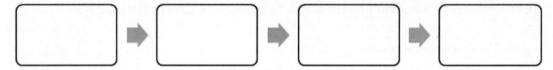

3.2.3 Note-taking skills

Taking effective notes in lectures and tutorials is an essential skill for university study. Good note-taking not only makes you listen attentively, but also represents your understanding of the whole listening material. Therefore, good note-taking allows a permanent record of key information that you can integrate with your own writing and use for exam revision.

The principles of note-taking are as follows: (1) be selective: decide what is important according to the speaker and your knowledge of the subject; (2) be brief: use abbreviations and symbols; (3) be clear: make sure the relationships between ideas are clearly related to each other.

With the principles of note-taking, here we introduce the forms, symbols, and abbreviations of note-taking.

3.2.3.1 Forms of note-taking

The listener is required to adopt a different form of note-taking when faced with a different information type so as to keep a retentive memory, to enjoy an effective review, and to have a further thinking, of what the speaker has said. The forms of note-taking visually leave us clear and organized information about the relationship of a concept, such as a mindmap, a table, and a flowchart. For example, a mindmap is often created around a single concept, drawn as an image in the center, to which associated representations of ideas such as images and words are added. Major ideas are connected directly to the central concept, and other ideas branch out from those. The following are some examples of note-taking forms.

- **A mindmap**

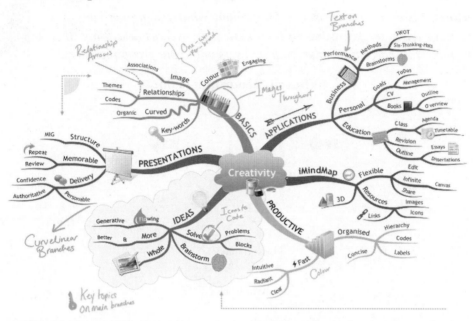

- **A table**

	Sound waves	Radio waves
Nature	mechanical	electromagnetic
Necessity of a medium	yes	no
Result from	changes in pressure in the medium	oscillations of the electromagnetic field

- **A flowchart**

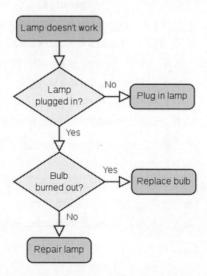

In-class exercise 3:

Directions: Listen to a professor talking about what geographers do, and write down the key words in the following flowchart describing their job. Then check and share your answers with your group members.

What do geographers do?

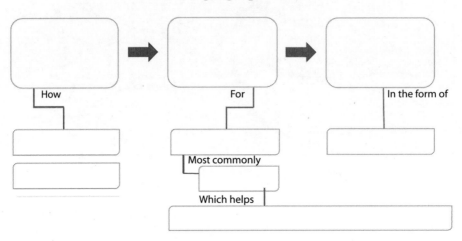

3.2.3.2 Symbols of note-taking

Symbols are characterized by brevity and convenience in order that the listeners can take notes effectively and quickly while listening. They can be mathematical symbols, arrows, punctuation marks, pictures or even personal symbols, but what is important is that they should be consistent and easy to remember. The following are some common types of symbols and examples.

- Mathematical symbols

Symbols	Meanings
∵	因为，由于，幸亏，because, due to, thanks to
∴	所以，结果，因此，therefore, so, consequently, as a result
=	相当于，等于，相同，equal, the same as
≠	不同，不等于，different, not the same
≈	大约，大致，相似，approximately, about, nearly
+	另外，还有，以及，in addition, and, what's more
>	超过，多于，更，more, bigger, exceed, surpass
<	少于，小于，不如，less, smaller
√	成功，同意，很好，正确，successful, agree, good, right
X	失败，错误，不好，不对，failure, wrong
△/*	特别，重视，重要，尤其，importance, especially, particular

- Arrows

Symbols	Meanings
←—→	稳定状态，静止, stationary condition, stability
→	将来，出口，前往，导致，提交, future, export, lead to, arrive in, send to, submit to
←	过去，进口，来自，源于, past, import, come from, originate in, result from
↑↗↘	增长，提高，发展，加强, increase, develop, improve, enhance, promote
↓↘↙	减少，下跌，恶化，降低, decrease, reduce, drop, deteriorate, lower, fall
↶	come back from, bring back from

- Punctuation marks

Symbols	Meanings
:	说, 告诉, 认为, 宣称, say, tell, believe, declare
?	询问, 疑问, 困惑, ask, question, doubt
●	观点, 论点, 点, 前/后, idea, point, last/next
( )	包括, 包含, including, within
…	等等, and so on
&	以及, 和, and, as well as, together with

- Pictures

Symbols	Meanings
$	金融, 钱, finance, money
口	口, 国家, mouth, country, nation
☉	国际, 全球, 地球, international, global
♂	男, man, male
♀	女, woman, female
☺	高兴, 喜悦, 满意, happy, pleased, satisfied
☹	难过, 沮丧, 不满, sad, depressed, unsatisfied

3.2.3.3 Abbreviations

There are certain forms of abbreviations for some words and phrases, such as *al.* for *although,* and *B.C.* for *before Christ.*

Abbreviations	Abbreviations
al. (although)	A. (answer)
B.C. (before Christ)	cf. (compare)
diff. (difficulty)	dept. (department)
ed. (editor)	e.g. (example)
edu. (education)	fund. (fundamental)
govt. (government)	info. (information)
Jr. (junior)	ltd. (limited)
lib. (library)	min. (minute)
nec. (necessary)	org. (organization)
poss. (possible)	Q. (question)
ref. (with reference to)	Ss. (students)
1st, 2nd, 3rd	Nov. (November), Oct. (October)

In-class exercise 4:

Directions: *Watch the video clip about Mona Lisa and take notes with symbols and abbreviations.*

3.2.4 Introductions in academic lectures

Suppose you are about to listen to a lecture, what do you expect the lecturer to talk about in the introduction part? The lecture introduction helps you predict the content or main ideas. The main functions of lecture introductions are as follows:

- Introduce the topic of the lecture;
- Define the scope of the lecture;

- Give background information about the topic;

- Provide an overview and content of the lecture.

When the lecturer makes an introduction, he/she usually takes language signals. There are two kinds of language signals that the lecturer tends to use. One is the signpost, and the other is transitional words. Signposts refer to words that indicate the moving of a lecture. To be alert to them will help you follow the lecture easily. Let's take a look at some examples.

- Introducing the topic of the lecture

  Today I'm going to take up the subject of...

  What I want to talk about is...

- Signaling a shift

  Now, let's move on to...

  Let's turn to the causes...

Transitional words refer to words and phrases which contribute to the understanding of the ideas as well as to the coherence of the lecture. Let's see the different functions of transitional words.

- Illustration: for instance, for example

- Cause: because, owing to, due to

- Effect: therefore, as a result, consequently

- Contrast: however, nevertheless, on the other hand

- Listing: first, in the first place, second, then

In-class exercise 5:

Directions: Listen to four audio clips and complete the table below.

Audio clips	Functions
	Introduce the topic.
	Define the scope.
	Give background information.
	Provide an overview.

In-class exercise 6:

Directions: *Listen to three audio clips and find out the signal words and their functions.*

(1) Signal words in audio clip 1: _____.

Function: _____.

(2) Signal words in audio clip 2: _____.

Function: _____.

(3) Signal words in audio clip 3: _____.

Function: _____.

3.2.5 Key ideas in academic lectures

To be an effective listener, you should learn to find the key ideas made by the speaker. The following are some clues that might help you pick out important ideas:

- The speaker often pauses before starting an important point;

- The speaker often uses repetition to emphasize the point;

- The speaker may change the pitch, volume and rhythm of their voice for emphasis;

- The speaker often uses introductory phrases to precede an important point;

- Some speakers use facial expressions or body movements when they are emphasizing a point.

Usually, there are lots of information in an academic lecture or a speech. Some are key ideas, and some are supporting details. Supporting details are statements that support a speaker's topic or theme. They may support their main idea by describing it, defining it, or otherwise giving information about it, regardless of how a speaker structures his reports, lectures, and so forth. The major and minor supporting details provide a variety of information essential to understanding and developing the argument.

How to distinguish key ideas from supporting details? Supporting details are often presented in the forms of description or definition.

In-class exercise 7:

Directions: *In this interview, Henry gives advice on how to deal with teenage children. Before you listen, read the following advice that is commonly given to parents on this subject. Then listen and choose the key ideas from the list that Henry discusses.*

① Be a good role model. Show them how to behave well by behaving well yourself.

② Let them make their own decisions about fashion when they are ready.

③ Monitor their behavior.

④ Give them freedom to experiment and have fun, as long as the behavior is safe and legal.

⑤ Discuss everything with your children.

⑥ Set clear limits. Be clear about what they can and cannot do.

⑦ Listen to them the way you talk to them. Avoid the annoying language that your own parents used on you.

⑧ Leave your children alone. Trust that they will ask you for advice if and when they need it.

⑨ Make sure you know who your children's friends are.

Key ideas: _____

3.2.6 Terminologies in academic lectures

Speakers usually introduce new terminologies to their listeners during lectures. The terms they introduce often represent new and quite abstract concepts which can be difficult to grasp. Here are some tips to help their listeners understand new terms or concepts:

- Provide a number of extended examples;
- Give definitions;
- Contrast the new concept with one that is already familiar to the listeners;
- Explain how the term or concept works.

Let's listen to an audio clip.

The word "Anthropocene", for example, may puzzle listeners, since it's not commonly used. Usually, in the academic lecture, the speaker would adopt different techniques to make it understood to the listeners. For example, define it: "Anthropocene" is a new geological era, where humans are the predominant driver of change at a planetary level.

Knowing the techniques that the speaker uses to introduce new terms and concepts, listeners may still feel anxious, or even frustrated when hearing these words in the speech. The following are some tips about how to solve and tolerate the ambiguity caused by unknown words:

- Skip the word over if it does not hinder your understanding of the major points;
- Use contextual information, common sense and background information to guess the meaning of the word;
- Move on to the next part and listen attentively to the speaker if you fail to figure out the meaning of an important word.

3.2.7 Digressions in academic lectures

What is a digression? Sometimes a speaker might say something that departs from the central topic in a speech in order to liven up the talk, to attract the listeners' attention or for other reasons. This is called a digression.

Why might the speakers digress during their lectures? There are a number of reasons:

- To give a short definition of a new technical term;
- To give a reference to a book on the topic;
- To comment on the point they are making;
- To comment on events happening outside the lecture;
- To give general information about the course;
- To give a personal anecdote to illustrate a point.

How to identify digressions? Successful listeners have the ability to identify digressions, that is, they are able to recognize the start and end of digressions in a speech. Here are some expressions which signal the start of digressions:

- I remember once…
- That reminds me…
- By the way, …

When the speaker wants to end the digressions, he/she might say:

- So as I was saying…
- Anyway, where was I?
- Back to the point, …

When the speaker digresses, he/she would often speak more slowly, loudly or have a pause in order to arouse the listeners' attention and make the point clearly.

In brief, academic listening skills are essential when you participate in an academic lecture. These listening skills help you get the main ideas, organize the relationship between different points, and involve in the lecture. As a facilitating tool, practicing these listening skills will help you go further in your academic learning.

In-class exercise 8:

Directions: Watch the video clip and choose the best answer to each question.

(1) Which sentence is the start of the digression in this lecture?
   A. I'm going to talk about…
   B. But I would point out before I go on that…
   C. Sara Shettleworth has a superb chapter on…
   D. But if you seriously want to think about this area, …

(2) When does the lecturer return to the main idea?
   A. But I would point out before I go on that…
   B. Sara Shettleworth has a superb chapter on…
   C. But if you seriously want to think about this area, …
   D. Anyway, some of the best-known work…

(3) What is the function of the digression in this lecture?
   A. To give a short definition.
   B. To give a reference.
   C. To give general information about the research.
   D. To give a personal anecdote to illustrate a point.

3.3
Activities for academic listening

Here are two activities which help students practice and review listening skills.

Activity 1: Word-changing

Directions: Work in groups to follow the steps below.

• First, add, delete or replace only one letter in the given word. In the meantime, give the definition to the word by using their own words.

- Then, keep changing one letter in the second word, then to the next word until they cannot.
- Finally, each group reports their words to the whole class. In the reporting session, other students can stop the reporter when he/she makes a mistake. The group that has the most words wins.

For example:

bank (a place for keeping the money)

back (opposite to the front)

…

Activity 2: Reviewing poster

Directions: Work in groups of four to follow the steps below.

- First, write the topic of this unit on the poster.
- Then, write 1–2 points about the topic one by one in two minutes for each. No repetitive points are allowed.
- After all four students in one group write down their points, the poster will be passed on to another group.
- Students in the different groups are asked to add missing points or details.

For example:

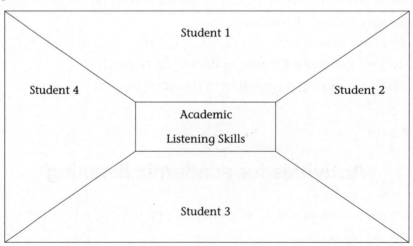

After-class tasks

❶ Consolidating quizzes

1. Listen to the audio and choose the best answer to each question.

(1) What does the speaker say about our teeth?
   A. They are highly sensitive to cold.
   B. They are vitally important to our life.
   C. They are a living part of our body.
   D. They are a chief source of our pain.

(2) What does the speaker say about plaque?
   A. It has to be removed in time by a dentist.
   B. It is a rare oral disease among old people.
   C. It contains many nerves and blood vessels.
   D. It is a sticky and colorless film on the teeth.

(3) Why is sugar harmful to teeth?
   A. It can change into acids, causing damage to their outer covering.
   B. It greatly reduces their resistance to the attacks of bacteria.
   C. It makes their nerves and blood vessels more sensitive to acid food.
   D. It combines with food particles to form a film on their surface.

(4) What causes adults to lose most of their teeth, according to the speaker?
   A. Food particles.　　　　　　　B. Gum disease.
   C. Unhealthy living habits.　　　D. Chemical erosion.

2. Review the note-taking skills learned in this unit, and then draw a mindmap to illustrate why plaque is the main enemy of healthy teeth.

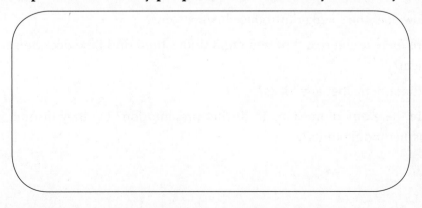

3. **Critical thinking:** Sugar is harmful to teeth, according to the listening passage. Do you like sweet food? Is there anything pleasant like sugar but actually harmful to your health in your life? If yes, how can you get rid of it?

(Points for references: advantages and disadvantages of having sugar; addiction to something that is fun may do harm to one's physical and psychological health; strategies for getting rid of some bad habits)

Ⅱ Mindmap

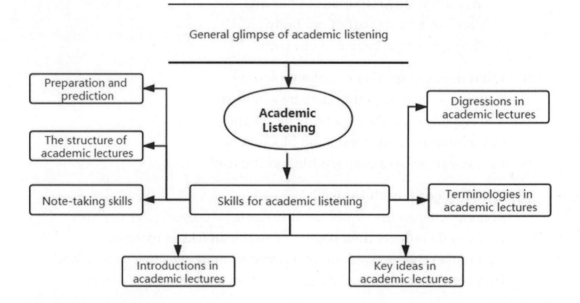

General glimpse of academic listening

- Academic Listening
- Preparation and prediction
- The structure of academic lectures
- Note-taking skills
- Skills for academic listening
- Digressions in academic lectures
- Terminologies in academic lectures
- Introductions in academic lectures
- Key ideas in academic lectures

Ⅲ Project task

In this unit, you are supposed to listen to one of your classmates' presentation carefully, take notes while listening and then give some suggestions. You can develop your project from the following perspectives:

- How does the speaker introduce his/her topic?
- Are there any terms that you don't understand and how does he/she explain them?
- What are his/her key ideas?
- Are there any digressions in his/her presentation? Do they distract you from his/her main points?

Ⓝ Extended resources

1. Further listening 1: An introduction to a lecture

Brief information: It is an introduction of a lecture on positive psychology, which mainly tells us what makes a happy life. And the lecturer tries to use the work of Mihaly Csikszentmihalyi and the theory of flow to give us answers. Finally, he gives us a detailed exploration of flow theory.

2. Further listening 2: A lecture about an experiment

Brief information: It is a lecture about a "pitch drop" experiment. This experiment was created by Professor Thomas Parnell, and he wanted to show that everyday materials, such as pitch, can have quite surprising properties. Only nine drops of the pitch have fallen from the glass funnel since 1927, and unfortunately Professor Parnell died without seeing a pitch drop. Today there's a live web stream that allows anyone to watch the glass funnel and wait for the fateful moment.

3. Video watching: Taking notes while listening

Brief information: It is an introduction to some tips of taking notes while listening.

Unit 4

Academic Communication

A very important aspect of any research project is to make your idea heard or known by others through publishing articles or giving oral presentations. To better interact and communicate with other researchers, you should share your ideas of what has been explored or show your results to the people working in the same field effectively.

If you want to improve your research ability and get inspired, you need not only to read more but also grasp every opportunity to join in a lecture or symposium. A symposium especially gathers experts from all over the world and enhances academic communication. They will bring most frontal ideas of scientific and technical developments in the related areas. So don't miss it.

Many of you may feel hard to understand a plenary lecture or a paper presentation in a symposium. There are some tips for you on how to understand the lecture or presentation in this chapter. Besides, you can also learn how to chair a conference, introduce a speaker, give a paper presentation, deliver a poster presentation, raise and answer questions, and employ visual aids. Now let's start our exciting journey.

Pre-class tasks

❶ Suggested MOOC resources

You can scan the QR code to get a general idea of what academic communication involves and different types of academic presentation.

- Paper presentation
- Poster presentation
- Chairing a conference
- Question and Answer session
- Project presentation

❷ Pre-quizzes

1. **Which of the following is NOT to be predicted while you are listening to an academic lecture?**

A. The general idea of the listening material.

B. The questions that might be raised after listening.

C. The best answers to the questions among the choices given.

D. The same words or phrases appearing in the answers.

2. **Which of the following is NOT the feature of an academic presentation?**

A. Insight and originality.   B. Gesture.

C. Scientific and logical content.   D. Time limitation.

3. **What elements are generally included in a paper presentation?** (*There may be more than one correct answer.*)

A. Title.   B. Introduction.   C. Body.   D. Conclusion.

4. **Which of the following are necessary when you are chairing a conference?** (*There may be more than one correct answer.*)

A. To confirm the speaker's information.

B. To orient the speaker to timing procedures.

C. To prepare some questions to stimulate discussion.

D. To ask questions before the speaker starts his presentation.

5. Which of the following statements will be the right response if you face a question you don't know in a Question and Answer session?

A. That is not a good question.

B. Can you ask another question?

C. I'm sorry. I don't happen to know the answer to that question.

D. I'm sorry, but I don't want to answer your question.

In-class tasks

4.1

General glimpse of academic communication

If you attend an institution of higher education or any academic programs, you can use some skills to contribute to the academic conversation with your teachers and peers. In order to help you better state your ideas, structures and methods adopted in different academic programs, it is a must for you to know how to start your journey of academic communication effectively.

Academic communication involves presenting ideas effectively and formally in a scholastic environment. It includes the words and structures used to express ideas, as well as the methods by which ideas are disseminated. In this unit, it particularly refers to oral communication by means of academic presentations. Therefore, all will be mainly discussed in terms of academic presentations rather than academic communication. An academic presentation is the process of stating an idea to the audience, which is typically a demonstration, introduction, lecture, or speech meant to inform, persuade, inspire, motivate, or build good will or to present a new idea or product. Presentations in certain formats are also known as keynote addressing.

The purpose of academic presentations is to present and discuss researchers' work and findings. Together with academic or scientific journals, conferences provide an important channel for the exchange of information between researchers.

Now let's look at the features of academic communication.

In academic communication, we have a more focused audience that comes to listen with a more specific purpose. Audiences are more likely to interact with presenters. As a result, we may have a different language style in academic communication compared with that of research papers. In addition, oral communication involves more complicated interaction, including speech presentation and non-verbal communication.

Specifically, the following are the general features of academic communication:

- Insight and originality

Presentation in academic communication requires not only the scientific nature of the content but also the insights that have a certain degree of originality.

- Scientific and logical content

In science disciplines, presenters in academic communication usually base their talks on visual presentations that display key figures and research results. They will also show some figures or results of their experiments and then analyze what those data mean in the discussion. This is a very common way to talk about their conclusion based on the data analysis.

- Language style

In academic communication, presenters have to consider that not all of the audiences are specialists, so the notes of terms presented on PPT slides may help a lot. Terms would be better understood if repeated several times. Simple sentence structures are preferred in a presentation.

- Time limitation

Oral presentation at an international academic conference is often given to introduce the research done and achievements made by the presenter in 20 or 25 minutes.

4.2

Types of presentations in academic communication

There are different types of presentations in academic communication. Based on the occasions that they are for, they can be classified as paper presentation, project presentation, poster presentation, and presentations in seminars. Whatever the types are, they are to present what you have found or achieved to the audience and communicate with them on the issues of the field.

4.2.1 Paper presentations

A way to make your ideas disseminate is by publishing papers or giving oral presentations. Some of you might say writing and publishing papers are so nerve-wracking, let alone giving paper presentations. It may be more challenging for you to spread your idea and communicate with others in an academic setting. After you've done with your paper, you may wonder how you can turn it into a dynamic, informative, and enjoyable presentation. Paper presentation could be a way to spread your ideas and an opportunity to communicate with others. Let's get to learn different perspectives of paper presentation.

4.2.1.1 Structure of a paper presentation

A successful paper presentation needs to be well-structured. Its common structure goes like this:

1. **Title**

Take the title of your paper as the topic of your presentation.

2. **Introduction**

Select 3–5 points to illustrate your topic. Sometimes you may have a point or two related to the background or in terms of literature review. A common way to introduce them is to follow the Three Moves method, which means to cover these points in your presentation, namely background, niche, purpose and significance.

3. **Body**

You may list your findings or results in this part. Remember to rank them according to the significance.

In the body part, we need to bear the following five things in mind:

- Present your main points one by one in a logical order (like chronological order, or hierarchical order) and use signal words to indicate where you are.

- Keep to the main points and avoid excessive details.

- Pause at the end of each point to give the audience time to take notes or time to think about what you are saying.

- Use examples or anecdotes to illustrate your point whenever you find it difficult or abstract for the audience to understand.

- Use analogies. If possible, make a comparison between the content of your presentation and the knowledge the audiences already have.

4. Conclusion

Summarize or restate the points of the paper in one or two sentences. You can even make suggestions or pose a question in this part. Four things should be noted in conclusion:

- Let the audience know that you are approaching the end of the presentation by restating your purpose and presenting what you have achieved.

- Leave your audience with a clear summary of the main points you have covered in the talk.

- Thank the audience. End your talk by saying "Thank you". Like most rituals, the thanks-applause sequence comforts everyone.

- Give the audience a chance to ask questions, using sentences like "Thank you" and "Are there any questions?".

4.2.1.2 Tips for paper presentations

1. Tell a story

Stories are one of the best ways to grab your audience's attention because a good story will arouse the audience's interest. Keep your story within 90 seconds, and then continue with your presentation. Now let us enjoy two examples about how a story works in a presentation.

In the first example, the speaker uses a story that happened at the dining hall to provoke the same feeling, the feeling of belonging, of all the audience that we are all members of the university.

In the second example, the speaker uses an interesting story of himself to arouse the audience's curiosity of how the story would be related with the topic, and another incident of his continues calling the same crazy feeling until we hear "If ever you feel weighed down by the bureaucracy, or often mundanity of modern life, don't fight the frustration. Let it be the catalyst for whimsy."

2. Ask your audience a question

Inviting your audience to participate in your presentation from the start will get them interested in your subject. You could ask a rhetorical question to stimulate their thought processes and prepare them for the rest of your presentation. For instance, if you are to talk about anti-oxidation, you can raise a question like, "Have you ever taken any pills or used any cosmetics on your skin to stay young?" The audience may have the background in anti-oxidation, so it can arouse their interest in the topic.

3. Say something shocking

Sharing a shocking statistic or fact will grab your audience's attention and hold them on the topic from the very beginning. For example, the speaker may start the presentation with a figure like "Every year, about 40% women aged 17–50 conducted a certain kind of plastic surgery." Why are women so obsessed with plastic surgery? With such an astonishing figure, the audience does want to know the answer.

4. Share a meaningful quote

Make sure that the quote you choose is relevant to your topic. This tip is always employed at the beginning of the talk to call resonance or at the end of the talk to summarize it. For instance, you can use "Beauty is held in the eyes of the beholder" to start with your research on how physical appearance changes as time goes by and the scientific ways to keep young.

5. Keep to the main points and avoid excessive details

You don't want to overload your audience with fluff, forcing them to miss the important stuff.

- Summarize each key point into a sentence or a few key words;
- Highlight new points with a relevant image or phrase;
- Offer evidence from your research to support your argument;
- Show data to support your findings.

4.2.1.3 Sentence patterns for paper presentations

1. Start the presentation

- Today I am going to talk about…
- My topic this morning is…
- I would like to start by thanking…for inviting me to share my paper here.
- I thank you for giving me this opportunity to share with you…
- I am so honored to address you on the important…
- Thank you for the marvelous introduction. It is a great pleasure to be here with you to…

2. Start the introduction

- Let me start by telling a story on how I started the research.
- Let me start by saying just a few words about my background.
- Let me show you a shocking picture of…
- I should begin by quoting…
- In this presentation, I shall confine myself to…
- My presentation will address two of the issues…
- The presentation will focus on…
- I feel privileged to share with you a few thoughts on…
- It's my great pleasure to be here this morning to address you on the subject of…
- I would like to present…
- I would like to elaborate on…

3. Talk about the body of presentation

- I have divided my presentation into five parts. First, I'm going to state…; second, I will give a…; third, I will focus on…; then comes my conclusion…
- To address these questions, I would like to give my talk in four parts. First, a brief look into…Second, case analysis of…Third, discussion and conclusion…Fourth,…
- My talk is structured into four parts: Part I:… / Part II:… / Part III:… / Part IV:…
- I will highlight three issues in today's talk. The first is…

4. Present parts of discussion

- Let's look at…in the first part.
- The first thing I want to talk about is…
- A second and important point that I am to address is…
- Another point I would like to make is…

5. Shift to another topic

- I have presented you with…And now I would like to stress another issue…
- There are still a few points to be addressed. One has to do with…
- We have talked about…Here are some points related to…

- This brings me to my third point which has to do with…
- I would also like to take a few minutes to highlight…

6. Refer to others' talks

- Both of the speakers today made very good points on…
- The speakers this morning have emphasized…
- The previous speakers covered the issue I am working on, but they differ slightly in…

7. End a presentation

- Before concluding…, I would like to touch upon…
- I would like to end my speech by quoting from…
- In closing, I want to note that…
- My time is running out. I have to stop here. Any questions or comments?
- This is my talk on…I would be pleased to answer any question you may have.
- Thank you for your attention! Any questions or comments?
- I will stop here. If you are interested in my topic, you can reach me by…and my article will be released this summer.

4.2.2 Project presentations

4.2.2.1 Structure of a project presentation

Normally, a project presentation includes these elements:

- Title of the project: an introduction to your topic or the problem you've addressed. (1–2 mins)
- Background information: how the problem impacts the real world (such as how a better understanding of the issue can impact humans). (1–3 mins)
- Methods: your hypothesis, or what you expected to learn about through your experiment. (1–3 mins)
- Procedure: each step of your experiment's process. (1–2 mins)
- Results: the results of your experiment. (7–10 mins)
- Conclusion, or summary of what you have learned and whether your data supports your hypothesis. (1 min)

4.2.2.2 Tips for project presentations

In a project presentation, you are to show your results as well as persuade your audience to follow your idea or support your hypothesis. Hence it is important for you to deliver your presentation effectively. Here are some tips for you.

- Create notecards. Use your notecards primarily to help you practice your presentation and keep them on hand to make sure your presentation stays on the subject.

- Plan your demonstration in a flowchart or graphs. Visual materials of your experiment or your research topic can help engage your audience.

- Create a clear PowerPoint presentation if necessary. Make clearly labelled slides for each section and use large and legible fonts. Avoid including too much text on each slide, as your audience might be overwhelmed by trying to read it or just won't read it all.

4.2.2.3 Dubbing activity

Directions: *You are making a presentation on the project of bionic hand. Dub the video on what you have done and achieved (Scan the first QR code). The second video is a reference of how the bionic hand was designed and how it works (Scan the second QR code).*

4.2.3 Poster presentations

Do you know what academic posters are? Academic posters are also called research posters. They are widely used in the academic community, and most conferences include poster presentations in their programs.

We use academic posters to summarize the research concisely and attractively to help publicize the researcher's findings and generate more discussions on this research among his or her research field. A poster is usually a mixture of brief text with tables, graphs, pictures, and other presentation formats. At a conference, the researcher stands by the poster while other participants can come and view the presentation and interact with the researcher. So, what makes a good academic poster? A good poster will meet the guidelines for the specific event and match the knowledge base and interests of the audience. It will focus on the major findings that may impress your audience. A good poster will be clearly organized and readable. In addition, the poster should be able to stand on its own as a clear, logical presentation of your work, without any explanation from you.

The following are the elements included in a poster:

- Title;
- Collaborators (including you) and their institutions;
- Abstract;
- Background / literature review;
- Research question(s);
- Materials, approach or process;
- Results/conclusion;
- Future directions, especially if this is a research in progress;
- Acknowledgement;
- Contact information.

4.2.3.1 Tips for poster presentations

The following are some tips for making a poster presentation:

- Learn about the background of the audience before conducting a presentation. Create a content that is understandable to everyone.
- Provide a concise but step-by-step explanation of each aspect highlighted in the poster. Design the content by keeping the audience, time limits, and important aspects of the topic in mind.
- Practice your presentation in front of your poster several times. You can talk to your partners or friends and get some feedbacks from them.
- Identify in advance the location of your poster session and be sure to arrive early (at least 30 mins) to put up your poster.
- Be prepared to promote yourself. Consider bringing handouts and business cards for those who visit your poster.
- Don't be a wall-flower. Don't just stand there, waiting for people to come to the poster and ask you questions. Ask people if they would like to hear about your work, and then start speaking.
- Do not read the poster to the audience. Look around at your audience and make eye contact. When you explain the graphics, you can point at them, and then you need to face the audience. Look at one for a few seconds and then look at another.
- Speak clearly and slowly. The place is usually very noisy; you need to make

yourself heard by all the people around you. Use voice tones and gestures to strengthen your passion for the topic. The audience will feel your passion and get interested in your work.

- Involve the audience. Make them think, discuss, react, find out more, and take certain courses of action.

- Take feedback positively. It is the diversity of thoughts induced through feedback that eventually leads to improvised analysis, research and projects.

4.2.3.2 Sentence patterns for poster presentations

- Would you like to hear about my research in about two minutes or less?

- This research project was supported by…

- The main components of our project were…

- If you look at the results of our second experiment, you'll notice that…

- The next phase of our research is to…

- Do you have any questions?

- Thanks for your attention.

In-class exercises:

(1) **Directions:** *Watch the poster presentation, write down the sentence patterns that the speaker uses in his presentation, and put these sentence patterns in different categories according to the elements of a poster presentation.*

(2) **Directions:** *Watch the video on Roll to Roll Solar Cell Printer and design a poster based on what you have watched.*

(3) **Directions:** *Suppose you are to join in a competition with the poster you have designed, present you product with your poster to a potential customer.*

4.2.4 Presentations in seminars

Giving a presentation in a seminar is a great opportunity to share your knowledge and experience with other people. Public speaking sometimes can be daunting, but practice and preparation can minimize many of these anxieties. If you have well structured your presentation, you can give the talk perfectly.

4.2.4.1 Structure of presentations in a seminar

To make an effective presentation in a seminar, you need to pay attention to the following points.

1. State the research question you have created

A research question is what you attempt to answer in your presentation. Creating a research question will help you stay focused as you specify your topic. It can also serve as the starting point for your presentation and your thesis following-up as well.

2. Illustrate your process of collecting data

Tell your peers what methods you have used in your research, and then give a detailed description of instruments, experimental procedures and software you used to process your data.

3. Present your claims and research

List some key points to show what you have found in short sentences or key phrases.

4. Conclude your paper

State some possibilities for concluding your presentation:

- Synthesize what you have discussed;
- Explain why your topic matters;
- Return to your opening discussion.

5. Make acknowledgement and answer questions

Tell your audience who has worked with you if there is any and what help you have gained from your peers or the team. Meanwhile, get ready for the questions from your peers.

Now you have a general idea of how to give a presentation in a seminar. But how can you persuade others effectively? Now we will move on to how to make a convincing argument.

4.2.4.2 Tips for making convincing arguments

Learning to construct a solid argument and understanding the person you're arguing with will enable you to convince anyone of anything. But how can you have an efficient argument? You should pay attention to the following points.

1. Define the terms of the discussion

Give an authorized definition of what you want to talk about. This will function more powerfully and limit your research to a certain scope.

2. Develop your reasoning

You need to define and articulate the main points you're trying to make and back up your reasoning with vivid examples and evidence. Memorable and striking details will help you illustrate your points.

3. Provide relevant background information with handouts to guide your audience

Providing adequate background information or context will help you to guide your audience through your presentation.

In-class exercise:

Directions: Scan the QR codes to choose one of the presentations to watch carefully. Then write down what you have heard and make an oral summary of the presentation you have chosen.

4.3
Chairing a conference

Apart from giving presentations at an academic conference, another possible task will be chairing a conference. A good chairperson helps the conference to run smoothly and efficiently. The person who chairs a meeting can sometimes be referred to as the "facilitator". So gracefully chairing a conference will make different sessions of the conference into a nice chain. Let's learn how to chair a conference.

4.3.1 Procedure of chairing a conference

Chairing a conference is such a great honor. Knowing some rules on how to do it and what the general procedure is will make the conference go smoothly. Not every conference is the same, but they share some similarities. The following is the general procedure:

- Announce the opening of the conference;
- Introduce yourself;

- Give a welcome speech;
- Introduce the conference;
- Tell the rules;
- Introduce a presentation;
- Give a closing speech;
- Sum up the achievements made in the conference;
- Express gratitude to the organizing committee, participants, and speakers—all the people involved.

4.3.2 Tips for chairing a conference

The following are some tips for you:

- Meet the speakers beforehand and confirm their information—names (pronunciations), institutions, papers to be presented, and honors they intend to be introduced.
- Orient the speaker to timing procedures. Tell him or her how much time he or she is supposed to speak.
- Start the applause while the speaker is mounting the steps.
- Thank the speaker before you invite questions for him or her.
- Prepare some questions to stimulate discussion if the audience is quiet.
- Get ready to introduce another speaker.

Before a talk or a plenary presentation, the speaker, no matter how experienced he or she is, will feel nervous when speaking at a conference. As the chairing person, your introduction will set a comfortable scene for the speaker and hold the audience's attention. The following aspects should be paid attention to:

- Your opening sentences;
- The speaker's personal file;
- Academic achievements;
- Awards and honors;
- Topic of the presentation;
- Your story with the speaker.

4.3.3 Sentence patterns for chairing a conference

1. **Announce the opening of the conference**
- I'd like to call the conference to order.
- I am very pleased/honored/delighted to declare the…conference open.

2. **Introduce yourself**
- First of all, I'll introduce myself. I'm…from…
- I am…, chairman of this conference. This conference is organized by…and co-sponsored by…Foundation and other organizations.

3. **Give a welcome speech**
- On behalf of the…, I am very pleased to warmly welcome…to attend this great gathering.
- On behalf of the organizers, we have the honor and privilege to welcome you to…
- It is my pleasure to welcome you to the conference…
- On behalf of the organizing committee, I would like to welcome all members and guests to this special event for what will certainly be an exciting, enjoyable and educational experience.

4. **Introduce the conference**
- The goals of this conference are threefold.
- This conference will focus on the discussion of the various aspects of…
- The aim of this conference is to…

5. **Tell the rules**

There are some basic rules. First, please limit your presentation to 15 minutes. At the end of each presentation, there will be 5 minutes for discussion. At the end of the session we will have an open discussion on any of the papers presented.

6. **Introduce a presenter**
- The first paper this morning will be presented by Dr. Smith, professor of…at… University, and his topic is…
- The next presentation in this session is on…I would like to ask Dr. Goers to talk about this very important subject.

7. Keep the allocated time

- Sorry, the schedule is rather tight. We haven't any time for discussion, so we must go on to the following paper.
- Dr. Chen, I'm sorry, but we do have to move on; we are running short of time.
- Excuse me, sir, our time is quite limited, so I'm not willing but have to ask you to stop here. We may have another chance to discuss about the topic later.

8. Call on the participants to involve

- Are there any questions about Dr. Xi's talk?
- As we still have a few minutes left, may I ask if there are any questions and comments?
- Is there anyone who wishes to add something to Prof. Johnson's presentation?

9. Indicate a closing speech

- We are soon closing this seminar which has been a great success.
- We have come to the end of this conference.
- Now, with great joy and a mind reluctant to part, we get together again to declare that the conference has drawn to a successful close.

10. Evaluate the conference

- Let me congratulate you on the achievements of this conference.
- Please accept my congratulations on a successful conference.
- I am very encouraged by the success of this conference. This event has demonstrated that...

11. Sum up the achievements made in the conference

- In light of the specific objectives of the three-day conference, I should confess that this is a successful one as far as...
- The presentation of papers took place in covering different topics.
- All the presentations were very illuminating and informative. And the heated panel discussions were very stimulating and fruitful.

12. Express gratitude to the organizing committee, participants, and speakers—all the people involved

- I want to thank everybody who took part in the organization of this event.

- This conference is a success because of your efforts and participation.

- Again, I want to thank everyone for making the conference an outstanding success!

13. Express best wishes to the participants

- Thank you. I wish you a pleasant trip home.

- I wish you all a safe journey back home.

- And lastly, my friends, see you next year in New York and have a safe trip home.

4.3.4 Getting-to-know-someone activity

Directions: *Complete the following introductory remarks by translating the Chinese statements in brackets into English.*

① _____ (很荣幸向大家介绍今天的演讲人), Nancy Hunter Denney.

A former subscriber to everyone else's definition of "having it all", Nancy Hunter Denney resigned from her administrative duties in higher education in 1993 to begin her own business, raised her own children and lived a life according to her own priorities. She is ② _____ (是……的作者) *Life by Design: A Do-It-Yourself Approach for Achieving Happiness* and served as the editor and co-author of *Let Your Leadership Speak: How to Lead and Be Heard*, recently released.

Today's speaker has ③ _____ (出现在) ABC and NBC morning shows in Chicago and on numerous radio stations across the country promoting her inspiring messages on life and leadership. She is a frequent ④ _____ (主题发言人) at national, regional and state conferences in higher education and other non-profit organizations.

Nancy ⑤ _____ (获得硕士学位) from Bowling Green State University in Ohio and ⑥ _____ (以优异成绩毕业) for her PhD from Oswego State University in New York. ⑦ _____ (在……之前) becoming a professional speaker, Nancy served ten years in higher education student affairs administration.

⑧ _____ (请和我一起欢迎)—from the coast of Massachusetts—author, educator, business owner, wife and first mate, Nancy Hunter Denney.

4.3.5 Jigsaw puzzle

Directions: *Watch the video clip, and complete an item from the following databank of introducing a speaker. Then try to complete your databank by finding different friends with different items.*

Speaker's personal file	
Academic achievements	
Awards and honors	
Topic of the presentation	
Your story with the speaker(s)	

4.4
Question and answer

An academic conference is not complete without a Question and Answer session, which is also called Q&A session. As a questioner, you can get more information, clarify confusion and get inspiration for your own work. As a speaker, you have spent several hours preparing that twenty-minute paper presentation, but the effort that goes into answering queries about your paper is as important as writing and presenting the paper. The Q&A session provides an opportunity for fellow academics to critique your work, and in return, you are expected to show that you know what you are talking about. In addition, it forces you to think on your feet as you are likely to face a few unexpected questions.

In this unit, we will first learn how to invite and raise the question. When you finish your presentation, you can invite questions like this:

- So, let's throw it open to questions.
- Now I'd like to answer any questions, if you have any.
- Now I am ready to answer your questions, if any.
- I'd be glad to try and answer any questions.
- Are there any questions?
- Any questions?

If you are the audience, you can ask the speaker a question in this way:

- I want to ask Dr. Green a question.
- I have a question for Dr. Anderson.
- Mr. Smith, I have a question to ask you.
- There is a question I'd like to ask Professor Li.
- A question for Mr. Liu.
- One question, Dr. Wei.
- Could I ask you a question, Professor Li?
- May I venture to ask Prof. Zhang a question?

4.4.1 Types of questions

Specifically, there are four types of questions: questions for clarifying problems, for showing special interest, for raising different opinions, and for information hunting.

If you want to clarify a problem, you can say:

- I don't quite understand what you really mean by saying "…" Can you explain it again?
- I would like to ask you a question, or rather, make a request. Is it possible for you to show me again your last slide?

If you would like to show special interest in the work, you can say:

- I'm very much interested in your presentation today since the work we are going to start has some connections with yours. Now, would you please say a few more words about the…?
- Dr. Johnson, I was fascinated by your description of your study, but what will happen if…?

If you want to raise a different opinion, you may say:

- Perhaps we're looking at the problem from different viewpoints. To the best of my knowledge, what you say seems to be theoretically unclear in…For example, …Could you give us some further explanations on that aspect?
- I'm very interested in your presentation on the positive analysis of efficient market hypothesis. But to the best of my knowledge, your viewpoint that… seems to be unreasonable. I'm afraid that…Could you give us some further

explanations on that aspect?

If you'd like to hunt for more information, you can ask:

- Would you be so kind as to give me more information about the method of your experiment?
- As you mentioned in your talk, you're doing the experiments on...I'm not specialized in the subject, but I'm sure it will involve a rather complicated technological process. Would you mind telling us more about that?

4.4.2 Tips for answering questions

To answer questions properly, you can keep the following tips in mind, especially you can learn to use the referred sentence patterns.

First, to make sure you hear the question clearly, you can confirm it. And the following are some sentences often used:

- Are you saying...?
- You mean...?
- What was the last point, please?
- Sorry, I didn't catch that. Would you clarify that for me?
- I think that's a very good question. But, could you please be more specific?
- Sorry, I don't know what you mean by the word...

Second, to show your respect, it would be polite to welcome the question. You can refer to the following possible patterns:

- This is a very good question.
- Thank you for that question.
- I'm glad this question has been brought up.
- I appreciate that question.
- That is an interesting question.

Third, to answer the question, you may repeat the precious remarks. Sentence patterns are as follows:

- To answer your question, I will just repeat what I said in my talk...
- Concerning this point, I think I have touched on it in my speech...
- To answer your question, I'd like to repeat the third point of what I said just now. Well, I was saying...

- If you are interested in..., I would suggest you look them up in my manuscript on Page 7, which have been shown in my presentation.

Fourth, to save time, you may answer the question partially. The followings are sentence patterns that you can use:

- Since time is limited, I think I can only answer part of your questions...
- One of the questions you put forward is about..., which I think is very interesting. And now I'd like to answer the question with...
- All right, I'll now say a few words about my future consideration on the subject...And I think that might be the answer to your last question.

Fifth, to respond to a challenging question, you can refer to the following sentence patterns to give an appropriate reply:

- I'm afraid that our different views on the point may come from the different angles from which we're looking at the problem.
- Well, judging from your question, I can see that your understanding of my viewpoints seems to be somewhat different from my original intention.
- Our study has not come to an end. If you agree, I'll answer your question later.
- I think it will be possible to answer this question when more experiments are completed.

Sixth, to answer a question that you don't know, you can just say frankly that you can't answer it or pass it to another participant who is sure to answer it. You can use the following sentence patterns:

- I'm sorry. I don't happen to know the answer to that question, but I'll be happy to check into it for you.
- I'm sorry. I don't think I can answer your question.
- I wish I could answer your question, but unfortunately, I have no good answer.
- I'm not sure that I can answer your question. What I'm going to say is not quite an answer to your question.
- I think your question can be better answered by Professor Li.

Seventh, to an improper question, you can refuse to answer it directly. The following sentence patterns can be referred to:

- I appreciate your interest in my research, but I just don't want to talk about it now. Let's talk about something else.

- I'd rather not say.

- Why do you want to know...?

Eighth, to interact with the questioner, you can refer back to him/her after you answer the question. For example:

- Did I answer your question?

- Did I answer you satisfactorily?

- I don't know whether this answered your question.

- I hope this may serve as an answer to your question.

In-class exercise:

Directions: *Watch a video clip of the Q&A session and find out which answer you like best and explain why.*

4.5

Visual aids for academic presentation

Visual aids can be a very powerful tool to enhance the impact of your presentation. Words and images presented in different formats can appeal directly to your audience's imagination, adding power to your spoken words. There are many different types of visual aids, such as PowerPoint, boards, handouts, flip charts, videos, and artefacts or props.

4.5.1 Types of visual aids

4.5.1.1 PowerPoint

Microsoft PowerPoint is now probably the most commonly used form of visual aids. It can really help you in your presentation if used properly; however, it can have the opposite effect sometimes. Now, let's learn how to create good PowerPoint slides for academic presentation in terms of layout, bullet points, graphs/diagrams, animations, citations and references, etc.

Think of the layout of your PowerPoint as visual rhetoric that takes the main ideas of your speech and code them into symbolic points. The most effective layout depends on consistency. Be sure that bullet points, the length and color of the points, and the size of font are consistent. The size of font needs to be at least 32 to be visible on the projector. Selecting a layout from the design tab is the easiest way to maintain consistency in the size of font and color scheme.

Bullet points should emphasize key ideas, not the idea word for word. If the audience must move their eyes more than twice to read the point, there are too many words after the bullet. Keep the bullets short, to the point, containing only a couple of words. Do not exceed more than one sub point because the audience will get lost. The sub point should emphasize a main point, but not the information that should be explained by the speaker.

To maintain a professional appearance, moderate and subtle animations such as ascending and appearing can be used to attract the audience to a point. If animations are too flashy, they begin to distract the audience. The animation is most effective when used consistently. Citations appear credible in APA or MLA format at the bottom of the slide or directly after the information. References at the end of a slide show are not necessary unless specified by the professor. References are, however, required in the speech outline.

Remember that an academic presenter does not use PowerPoint slides to drive or present the speech word by word. Instead, he uses the slides to convey information, stay on track, and interpret the presented materials.

4.5.1.2 Boards

White or black boards can be very useful to explain the sequence of ideas or routines, particularly in sciences. Use them to clarify your title or record your key points as you introduce your presentation, and this will give you a fixed list to help you recap as you go along. Rather than expecting the audience to follow your spoken description of an experiment or process, write each stage on the board, including any complex terminology or precise references to help your audience take accurate notes. Check to make sure your audience has taken down a reference before rubbing it off—there is nothing more frustrating than not being given enough time!

4.5.1.3 Handouts

Handouts are incredibly useful. Use a handout if your information is too detailed to fit on a slide or if you want your audience to have a full record of your findings. Consider the merits of passing round your handouts at the beginning, in the middle and at the end of a presentation. Given too early, they may prove a distraction. Given too late, your audience may have taken too many unnecessary notes. Given out in the middle, your audience will inevitably read rather than listen. One powerful way of avoiding these pitfalls is to give out incomplete handouts at key stages during your presentation. You can then highlight the missing details vocally, encouraging your audience to fill in the gaps.

4.5.1.4 Flip charts

A flip chart is a large pad of paper on a stand. It is a very useful and flexible way of recording information during your presentation—you can even use pre-prepared sheets for key points. Record information as you go along, keeping one main idea to each sheet. Flip back through the pad to help you recap your main points. Use the turning of a page to show progression from point to point. Remember to make your writing clear and readable and your diagrams as simple as possible.

4.5.1.5 Videos, and artefacts or props

Videos give you a chance to show stimulating visual information. Use video to bring movements, pictures and sound into your presentation. Always make sure that the clip is directly relevant to your content. Tell your audience what to look for. Avoid showing any more film than you need.

Sometimes it can be very useful to use artefacts or props when making a presentation. If you bring an artefact with you, make sure that the object can be seen and be passed round a small group or moved to different areas of a large room to help your audience view it in detail. Remember that this will take time and that when the audiences are immersed in looking at an object, they will find it hard to listen to your talk. Conceal large props until you need them; they might distract your audience's attention.

Finally, always check your equipment to make sure that it works and it is the equipment you are familiar with. There is nothing worse than a presenter struggling with his visual aids. A confident use of visual aids will help integrate them into your spoken presentation and become part of an impressive performance.

We have talked about how to use visual aids—PowerPoint, white or black boards, paper handouts, flip charts, videos, and artefacts or props—to help deliver academic presentation. We have also learned to use visual aids to display complex information clearly and introduce variety into delivery techniques. Make sure that you are familiar with the equipment, and deploy visual aids creatively in your presentation to create an impact.

When you progress in your academic studies, you will increasingly understand that your fluency in academic oral communications plays an important role in your academic performance and future career. This unit will help equip you with effective communicating strategies, overcome common language challenges and build self-confidence when you participate in a range of different academic interactions.

4.5.2 Perfection activity

Directions: *Collect one of your friend's PowerPoint slides or poster. Make some comments and then offer suggestions to help him/her perfect the visual aids to achieve better performance.*

After-class tasks

❶ Consolidating quizzes

1. **Choose the best answer to each of the question.**

(1) To record the structure of a lecture in a clear way, you'd better use the blank space of your paper and indent the specific points.

A. True   B. False

(2) What techniques are usually used for introducing new concepts in an academic lecture?

A. Examples.   B. Definitions.   C. Contrasts.   D. Explanations.

(3) What are suggested doing in the conclusion of a paper presentation?

A. Restating your purpose.

B. Leaving you audience with a summary.

C. Showing thanks to your audience.

D. Encouraging your audience to ask questions.

(4) What are the effective ways to deliver a project presentation?

A. Creating notecards.

B. Making a PowerPoint presentation.

C. Making use of flowcharts and graphs.

D. Presenting the project as detailed as possible.

(5) A research question can serve as the starting point of a seminar presentation.

A. True　　　　　　　　　　　　B. False

(6) What are included in an academic poster?

A. Title.

B. Author's past experiences.

C. Materials, approach and process.

D. Results.

(7) It is effective to use PowerPoint to drive or present the speech word by word when you deliver an academic presentation.

A. True　　　　　　　　　　　　B. False

2. **Experience sharing: Have you ever attended a lecture or a symposium? What makes you go there? Give some suggestions to those who want to participate in a symposium.**

3. **Critical thinking: Many undergraduates believe that going to a conference or joining in a lecture is not what they need to do during their university life. Conferences mean more to graduates. Do you hold different ideas? Talk with your partners and deliver a speech with the information you collect.**

(Points for references: the latest research trends; popular and widely-accepted theory or methodology; inspired; opportunity to communicate; learn from peers; to broaden your international horizon)

Ⅱ Mindmap

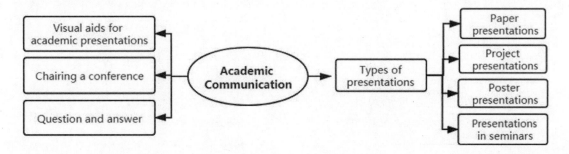

Ⅲ Project task

For this project, you are supposed to talk about an article you have read in your field or discuss your proposal in a workshop. You can develop your project from the following perspectives:

- A brief introduction to the the author's background or what sparkles your research on the topic;
- List the general structure of the research article;
- Focus on one part that differentiates it from other articles;
- Prepare questions and explicate your difficulties or doubts.

Ⅳ Extended resources

1. **Further learning: Watch the plenary presentation on the topic of "The Liquid Metal Battery".**

   Brief information: It is a presentation made by Donald R. Sadoway, from Department of Materials Science and Engineering, Massachusetts Institute of Technology. (Taken from Stanford University website.)

2. **Further paper reading: "A Study of Academic Oral Presentation Anxiety and Strategy Employment of EFL Graduate Students"**

   Brief information: The paper studies the different strategies that English majors and non-English majors employ. The main causes of anxiety are related to the content of the presentation, students' oral proficiency and their delivery skills. Some methods of reducing anxiety in academic oral communication are discussed in the paper.

Unit 5
Academic Vocabulary

EAP scholars and practitioners commonly classify some words as "academic" on the basis that they are used more frequently in academic settings than non-academic settings. Simply put, academic English refers to the oral, written, auditory, and visual proficiency required to learn effectively in schools and academic programs. It can be contrasted with everyday informal speech and other genres. And the academic words are usually not among the most frequent 2,000 words of English according to the General Service List.

Knowledge of academic words is essential to understand the academic text. Look at the title from a SCI journal paper: "Experimental Analysis of **Ethanol** Dual-Fuel **Combustion** in a Heavy-Duty **Diesel** Engine: An Optimization at Low Load."

This example demonstrates that the reader must have a vocabulary rich enough to support his/her understanding of the text. Here by "rich", we mean you need a large vocabulary base, including both general academic terms such as "experimental", "analysis", and "dual", and technical terms such as "ethanol", "combustion", and "diesel".

Here comes one more example: the word "basic" refers to "fundamental" in everyday English. However, it has a totally different meaning when used in the academic context. Thus, you need to be fully aware of that. "Basic" in chemistry refers to "of, having the nature of, or containing a base; alkaline".

Above all, you can only be viewed as part of a given science community with knowledge of those terms. But another question arises. On occasion, some terms are exclusively known to specialists. The only way for authors to explain what they mean in the context is paraphrasing. Therefore, in this unit you will be imparted with some knowledge to use paraphrasing techniques.

Apart from anything else, you will also strive to enlarge your academic vocabulary and learn dictionary skill. For example, you'll learn more about the fundamentals like specific chunks of words, which are prefixes, suffixes and compound words. Likewise, you will have a glimpse of tools like the corpus, which allow those with an interest in language a new way of looking at language. The corpus is a large and structured set of texts, nowadays electronically stored and processed. "Corpora", the plural form of "corpus", allow learners to quickly and easily see how professionals use the texts in journal papers.

Thanks to the innovative technology, you will be able to carry out the analysis of language in real academic contexts. And above all, you can get to know the frequency of words and phrases in Sci/Tech section of the corpus, and you can also easily see what words are the most representative. After learning this unit, you can work out these questions: What's the frequency of a word in a discipline? What is the collocation of a given word? How is it different from a synonym?

Pre-class tasks

❶ Suggested MOOC resources to learn

You can scan the QR code to expand your academic vocabulary using word formation techniques such as prefixes, suffixes and compound words as well as the paraphrasing and dictionary skill: corpus.

- Prefixes in academic vocabulary
- Suffixes in academic vocabulary
- Other types of words in academic vocabulary
- Paraphrasing
- COCA (Corpus of Contemporary American English)
- AntConc (A corpus analysis toolkit)

❚ Pre-class quizzes

1. **What is the meaning of the word "biodiversity"?**

A. A gas, liquid, or solid from natural sources such as plants that is used as a fuel.

B. The branch of biology concerned with the geographical distribution of plants and animals.

C. The science which is concerned with the study of living things.

D. The existence of a wide variety of plant and animal species living in their natural environment.

2. **What is the meaning of the word "erosion"?**

A. Removal of rock and soil.

B. Infiltration of rock and soil.

C. Penetration of rock and soil.

D. Formation of rock and soil.

3. What is the meaning of the compound word "sugar-free"?

A. Free sugar.

B. Without lactose.

C. Not containing sugar.

D. Wasteful of sugar.

4. **What does the acronym AWL refer to?**

A. American English Word List.

B. Academic Word List.

C. Academic Writing Learners.

D. American English Writing Lessons.

5. **Which of the following cannot be done with "List" in COCA?**

A. searches: *-friendly

B. customized word lists: @clothes

C. synonyms: =beautiful

D. compare: utter and sheer

In-class reading

5.1
General glimpse of academic vocabulary

Academic vocabulary is difficult to define. One broad definition is the vocabulary which can be used in academic contexts. The contexts can vary from spoken contexts (e.g. lectures, seminars, and presentations) to written ones (e.g. essays, papers, and reports).

In general, academic vocabulary consists of three types: general vocabulary which is acceptable for academic use, non-general academic vocabulary, and technical vocabulary specific to an individual subject area.

5.1.1 General vocabulary which is acceptable for academic use

General vocabulary may have special meaning in academic contexts. Let's take "meaia" and "excite" as examples.

In general, "media" refers to the means of communication that reach large numbers of people, such as television, newspapers, and radio; while in sciences, it refers to a substance that something grows in, exists in, or moves through. For example, "More direct approaches in highly acidic media have shown promise at small scale but not cost-effective."

In general, "excite" means to make someone feel happy and enthusiastic about something good that is going to happen; while in sciences, if something excites a feeling or reaction, it makes people or something feel or react in that way. For example, "The resultant individual oxygen atoms electrically excite surrounding molecules, producing nightglow."

5.1.2 Non-general academic vocabulary

Researchers have long been interested in creating a list of words which are not explicit enough for students to learn in secondary-school study, but which are frequent in all or most academic disciplines and can therefore be studied by all EAP learners. Perhaps the most well-known example of such a list is the Academic Word List (AWL) by Coxhead (2000). This can be a useful resource for building general academic vocabulary, though it should be remembered that this list is derived from written academic texts, so this list is most useful for written contexts. (You can scan the QR code to check the AWL.)

A recent list is the New Academic Word List (NAWL), which seeks to create a more updated list of academic words, since it is founded on the New General Service List (NGSL) from 2013, in contrast to the AWL which is founded on the General Service List (GSL) dating from 1953.

There are two other commonly used lists for academic English. One is called the Academic Collocation List, which commonly uses collocations in written academic texts (e.g. "elegant analysis"). The other is called the Academic Formulas List, which commonly uses formulaic sequences in academic English (e.g. "with regard to").

5.1.3 Technical vocabulary specific to an individual subject area

Each subject (mathematics, physics, etc.) has vocabularies which are either used specifically in that subject area (and not in general English), or common words which are used with special meaning in that subject area. Such words are known as technical, domain-specific or subject-specific words. The following are examples of non-general words used in the subject area of chemistry:

- **multiquantum**: the constitution of many smallest amounts of a physical quantity that can exist independently, especially a discrete quantity of electromagnetic radiation.
- **phosphate**: a chemical compound that contains phosphorus, which is often used in fertilizers.

Some technical words can be difficult even for native speakers to learn, though they may have some advantages in recognizing prefixes, suffixes, or roots, which may indicate the word meaning; for example, "multi" in "multiquantum" means "many".

5.2

Lexical features in a morphological sense

It is evident that both the grammatical and lexical features are distinctive in academic English. But in the subject area of science and technology, the difference would seem to be predominantly lexical. Thus, some knowledge and rules of the morphological formation of words are quite essential to your learning.

5.2.1 Prefixes of academic words

Prefixes are word parts that are attached to the beginning of a word to produce a related word. They usually change the meaning rather than the part of speech. Although most prefixes are Latin in origin, many come from Greek or Anglo-Saxon, with the result that there may be more than one prefix with the same meaning. For example, "uni-" (from Latin) and "mono-" (from Greek) both mean one, as in "universe" (everything that exists) and "monolingual" (one language). What's more, some prefixes with the same meaning and origin have more than one form, often because of spelling rules and the sounds which follow them. For example, the negative prefix "in-" becomes "im-" when followed by "m" or "p" (e.g. "immortal" and "import"), "il" when followed by "l" (e.g. "illegal") and "ir-" when followed by "r" (e.g. "irregular").

The following are some common academic prefixes meaning negation.

Category	Prefixes	Meanings	Examples
negation	anti-	against	**anti**biotic/**anti**body
	de-	opposite	**de**construct/**de**cline
	dis-	opposite	**dis**tribution
	in-/im-	opposite	**in**ability/**im**probable
	mis-	incorrect	**mis**information
	non-	not	**non**-existent/**non**-biased
	un-	opposite	**un**like/**un**known

Let's see an example.

> Pulsars are spinning, magnetized neutron stars that are observed as a regular sequence of radio pulses. Most pulses are of consistent intensity, but occasionally one is brighter by orders of magnitude. The cause of these unpredictable giant radio pulses (GRPs) is **unknown**. Enoto et al. observed the Crab Pulsar simultaneously with X-ray and radio telescopes. They found that X-ray emission during GRPs was slightly brighter than that during normal pulses. Comparing the radio and X-ray enhancements provides constraints on the GRP emission mechanism and the possible connections with other transient radio phenomena. (Smith, 2021)

From the example above, we can easily recognize the research question in an abstract with the help of the prefix meaning "not or opposite": "The cause of these unpredictable giant radio pulses (GRPs) is unknown", we know immediately that the purpose of the study is to investigate the cause of GRPs.

The following are some common academic prefixes meaning bad.

Category	Prefixes	Meanings	Examples
quality	dys-	bad	**dys**function
	mal-	bad	**mal**function
	anti-	against	**anti**biotics/**anti**body
	contra-/conter-	against	**contra**ry/**counter**part
	syn-/con-/co-	with	**co**-exist/**co**-author

Let's see another example.

> DNA methylation was one of the first epigenetic mechanisms discovered, but there is a limited understanding of its regulation and **dysregulation** in the context of development and disease. Dixon et al. performed a genome-wide CRISPR-Cas9 screen in human embryonic stem cells to identify DNA methylation regulators (see the Perspective by Gu and Goodell). A top screen hit, QSER1, proved to be essential for maintaining low methylation at DNA methylation valleys, which overlap with developmental genes and broad H3K27me3 and EZH2 peaks. Mechanistic examination revealed that QSER1 and the demethylating enzyme TET1 cooperate to safeguard developmental programs from de novo methylation by the enzyme DNMT3. (Purnell, 2021b)

In the example above, the prefix "dys-", meaning "bad" in quality in this abstract, may send the signal to skilled readers that they need to relate the sentence to the research question. This kind of connection may facilitate readers, in particular non-native speakers, with things like signposts.

There are also some other common prefixes of academic words.

In academic English, several other categories of prefixes meaning "number", "position" and "quantity" are also quite essential to your word building.

Category	Prefixes	Meanings	Examples
number	hemi-/semi-	half	**hemi**sphere/**semi**conductor
	mono-	one	**mono**poly
	di-/bi-	two	**di**chotomy
	tri-	three	**tri**ple/**tri**angle
	deca-/deci-	ten	**deci**mal
	mega-	million	**mega**byte
	poly/multi-	many	**poly**technic/**multi**ple
position	ex-	out	**ex**ternal
	exo-/extra-	outside	**exo**genous/**extra**ordinary
	in-	inside	**in**sight
	inter-	between	**inter**nal/**inter**vention
	sub-	under	**sub**sequent/**sub**stantial
	under-	under	**under**lying
	trans-	across	**trans**ition/**trans**mission
	peri-	around	**peri**pheral/**peri**meter
	circum-	around	**circum**stance/**circum**ference
	pro-	forward	**pro**ceed
quantity	hyper-	extreme	**hyper**activity
	over-	too much	**over**work
	re-	again	**re**view
	out-	more/better	**out**come/**out**line
	ultra-	more	**ultra**sound/**ultra**violet

Among others, some prefixes are only very common in sciences. The following is a short list of them. You can use corpus for reference and add your own examples.

Prefixes	Meanings	Example	More examples
a-/an-	without	**an**aerobic	
amphi-	both sides	**amphi**bian	
auto-	self	**auto**-immune	
bio-	life	**bio**logy	
carcin-	cancer	**carcin**ogen	
dia-	across	**dia**meter	
electro-	electricity	**electro**dynamic	
epi-	upon	**epi**dermis	
hydro	water	**hydro**geology	
kine-	move	**kine**tic	
macro-	large	**macro**scopic	
strat-	layer	**strat**osphere	

5.2.2 Suffixes of academic words

Suffixes are morphemes (specific groups of letters with particular semantic meaning) that are added to the end of root words to change their part of speech. Broadly speaking, suffixes can be classified into inflectional and derivational ones. Unlike inflectional suffixes that are only used to modify the grammatical meaning of a word (for example, the suffix "-s" is used with most nouns to indicate that they are plural), in many cases, the word formed by the addition of a derivational suffix will belong to a completely different part of speech.

Suffixes	Roof words	Derivatives	More examples
-al	region	region**al**	
-ary	caution	caution**ary**	
-ic	photograph	photograph**ic**	

(Continued)

Suffixes	Roof words	Derivatives	More examples
-ical	alphabet	alphabet**ical**	
-less	power	power**less**	
-like	war	war**like**	
-ly	cost	cost**ly**	
-ous	poison	poison**ous**	
-able/-ible	expand	expand**able**	
-ant/-ent	differ	differ**ent**	
-ed	bore	bor**ed**	
-en	prove	prov**en**	
-ive	create	creat**ive**	
-ing	tell	tell**ing**	

In addition to changing nouns/verbs to adjectives by adding suffixes, we can also add some common science suffixes to form nouns. You can complete the following table with more examples.

Suffixes	Meanings	Examples	More examples
-arium	place for	aqu**arium**	
-cide	killer of	pesti**cide**	
-cule	very small	mole**cule**	
-en	made of	wood**en**	
-ist	one who practices	scient**ist**	
-itis	infection	laryng**itis**	
-let	small	plate**let**	
-ment	action or process	experi**ment**	
-ology	study of	bi**ology**	
-osis	process	osm**osis**	

(Continued)

Suffixes	Meanings	Examples	More examples
-phyll	plant	chloro**phyll**	
-ize	to make	synthe**size**	
-oid	resembling	aster**oid**	
-tude	state of	ampli**tude**	

5.2.3 Compound words

In simple terms, a compound word is a word made up of two or more words, which are put together to form a new meaning. Compound words usually fall into the following four categories: "Noun + Adjective", "Adjective + Adjective", "Noun + Noun" and "Noun/Adjective + Verb" .

5.2.3.1 Noun + Adjective

accident-prone: a lot of accidents

sugar-free: not containing sugar

carbon-neutral: not affecting the total amount of carbon dioxide in the atmosphere

computer-aided: computer assisted

power-driven: powered by an electric motor

self-generated: made without the aid of an external agent

custom-built: built according to someone's special requirements

5.2.3.2 Adjective + Adjective

heavy-loaded: a large quantity of things into something

quick-frozen: rapid refrigeration at the temperature of 0 °C or lower

5.2.3.3 Noun + Noun

air-crew: the pilot and other people who are responsible for flying a plane and for looking after any passengers who are on it

play-group: an informal school for very young children, where they learn things by playing

chat-room: a site on the Internet, or another computer network, where users can post messages and read messages posted by other users

5.2.3.4 Noun/Adjective + Verb

spot-check: to examine one thing from a group

short-circuit: electricity travels along the wrong route and damages the device

hot-press: a machine for applying a combination of heat and pressure to give a smooth surface to paper, to express oil from it, etc.

5.3
Lexical features in a pragmatic sense

In a range of institutional and professional domains of an academic kind, all uses of language are specific in purpose in that they are associated with different discourse communities and users (a group of members with shared knowledge, values and conceptualization of things). Then what is also at stake is not what is proper in terms of the word formation but how words are put to appropriate contextual use. That is to say, words take on different meanings from their general meaning, but more importantly, the choice of words is regulated by institutional and professional genres (culturally informed ways of thinking and communicating). The extensive body of studies in English for specific purposes has drawn on the findings of genre analysis to identify the particular conventions for language use in certain professional domains.

5.3.1 Abstract reading and vocabulary analysis

Although humans show minimal regenerative capability, zebrafish can regenerate their hearts through **a mechanism** whereby heart muscle cells (cardiomyocytes) revert to a less mature state and then proliferate to replace the damaged tissue. Ogawa et al. show that Krüppel-like factor 1 (Klf1/Eklf), a transcription factor well known for its role in red blood cell development, is an essential factor for heart regeneration in zebrafish. Klf1 is specifically expressed in cardiomyocytes after injury, and its activation is sufficient to stimulate new cardiomyocyte production without injury. This potent effect is achieved through reprogramming of gene networks regulating cardiomyocyte differentiation and mitochondrial metabolism. (Purnell, 2021a)

In everyday English, native speakers tend to use "way", "means", "method", "procedure", etc. to indicate a process to make things done. However, in the abstract above, the author uses "mechanism" to express the meaning of "way". In *Collins Dictionary*, "mechanism" is defined as "a special way of getting something done within a particular system" and it has been acknowledged that "mechanism" is used to substitute "way" in academic settings. The following are more illustrations of the use of the word "mechanism".

- The carbon-oxygen bonds that hold alkyl ethers together are relatively inert. Lyu et al. report that zinc and nickel can team up to insert boron between the carbon and oxygen using an unusual **mechanism**.
- Comparing the radio and X-ray enhancements provides constraints on the GRP emission **mechanism** and the possible connections with other transient radio phenomena.
- To be able to treat more patients effectively or to treat patients who are most likely to respond, it is important to understand the **mechanism** of these agents.
- DNA methylation was one of the first epigenetic **mechanisms** discovered, but there is a limited understanding of its regulation and dysregulation in the context of development and disease.
- These experiments are consistent with a **mechanism** starting with electron transfer from the fatty acid to a photoexcited oxidized flavin cofactor.
- The authors examined its **mechanism** of action and demonstrated how it can be targeted to expedite the killing of BRCA1-mutant cancer cells in combination with PARP inhibitor treatment.

5.3.2 Academic Phrasebank

To sum up, we should make it grammatically and pragmatically correct when using academic vocabulary. But for beginners, it is really complicated to conform to those conventions. Thus, we may need some tools to remedy this situation. Of course, some online resources are available to academic readers and writers. Among others, Academic Phrasebank is one of the useful resources, since it can prepare us for a variety of templates in different sections of research articles.

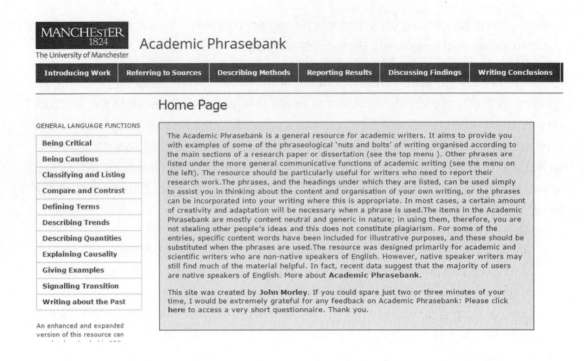

5.3.3 Paraphrasing

5.3.3.1 The definition of paraphrasing

What is paraphrasing? When do we use paraphrasing? And how do we paraphrase? Let's answer the questions in details.

To start with, what is paraphrasing? It is a way of reproducing a short section of text, such as phrases and sentences. It involves restating, interpreting or clarifying another person's idea in one's own words.

When do we use paraphrasing? Paraphrasing is used when we express another person's ideas in our own words; when we avoid copying another person's words; when we show how we understand the original text; and when we use it as an alternative for quotation.

5.3.3.2 Strategies for paraphrasing

1. Use semantic paraphrasing

Use your own knowledge to replace words in the passage with accurate synonyms. Make sure that the synonyms you use in your paraphrased version do not change the original meaning of the passage.

For example, "Food can be **produced** much more **cheaply** today **because of improved** fertilizers and **better** machinery." We can replace the bold words with "manufactured", "economically", "thanks to" and "advanced" respectively. Then the paraphrased version is: "Food can be **manufactured** much more **economically** today **thanks to advanced** fertilizers and machinery."

2. Use syntactic paraphrasing

Change the structure of the original sentence either by changing the order of sentence parts, breaking them into shorter sentences, or by combining simple sentences into compound and complex sentences.

For example, we can change the passive voice "Food can be produced" in the example above into the active voice "People can manufacture food".

Here is another example, "Obviously then, an insect that lives on wheat //can build up its population to much higher levels on a farm //devoted to wheat// than on one in which wheat is intermingled with other crops." We can paraphrase this long sentence by breaking into shorter sentences in our own words without changing its meaning. Then the paraphrased version is: "On a plot, only wheat is grown, and on another plot wheat and other crops are mixed together. The number of insects living on the former will become bigger than those living on the latter."

We can also combine simple sentences into compound and complex sentences. For example, "The cause of autism has also been a matter of dispute. Its incidence is about one in a thousand. And it occurs throughout the world."

There are three simple sentences in the example and we can combine them into a compound sentence. Then the paraphrased version is: "It has been controversial in the cause of autism, which occurs in one out of every thousand children across the world."

Successful paraphrasing requires a large vocabulary base and your competence of comprehension. It's also significant to keep the original meaning and make sure of its correctness and completeness. In addition, a proper paraphrasing will demand the change of structure, particularly for long and complex statement(s). Otherwise, your words might be considered as plagiarism. Usually, the change of structure will be considered first before you use different words.

5.4
Dictionary skill for academic vocabulary learning

Dictionary skill here doesn't refer to the ability to use dictionary effectively and efficiently, it means the effective use of corpus. A corpus is a large collection or database of machine-readable texts involving natural discourse in diverse contexts. It can enhance second language learning. Perhaps the best argument in favor of using corpus is that corpus-aided language learning can provide us with adequate and authentic examples of word-building, collocation and appropriateness. Now we will introduce several corpora for you.

5.4.1 Corpus of Contemporary American English (COCA)

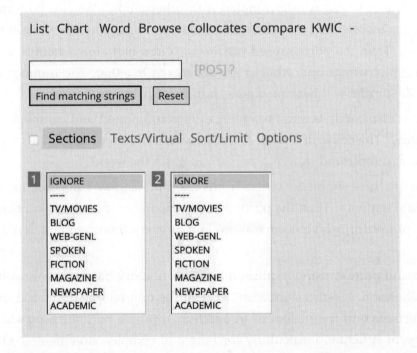

- "List": You can search any words and they will be displayed in the context. Or you can search part of a word (prefix, root or suffix) and words with those roots or affixes will be displayed in the order of frequency.
- "Chart": The option shows the total frequency of a word in academic or

everyday English section.

- "Collocates": The option enables us to accurately find what usually occurs with the key word you want to use.

- "Compare": The option can allow us to see how two confusable words differ in meaning and usage.

5.4.2 AntConc

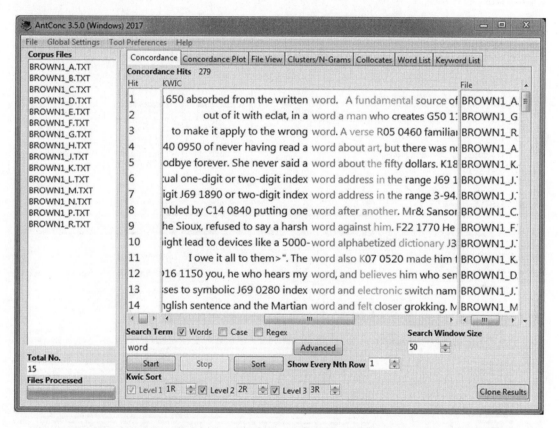

The freeware corpus analysis toolkit can allow you to custom-build your own corpus to analyze how a specific word is used in your chosen texts. Considering all the tools, it's essential to learn to generate "word list" of your own corpus and make use of "concordance tool" to see how words and phrases are commonly used in texts you import in the software.

5.4.3 RCPCE & MICUSP

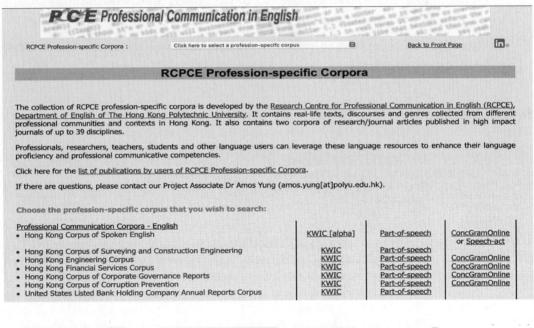

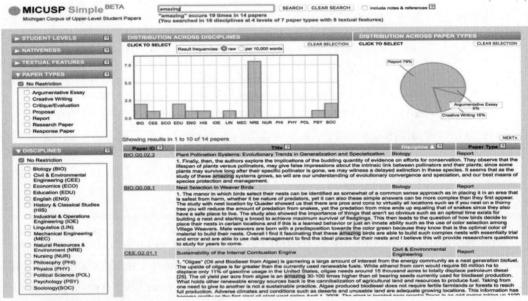

These two profession-specific corpora are subject-specific. RCPCE is the collection of papers of high-impact factors in disciplines ranging from civil and structuring engineering to land surveying and geoinformatics, while MICUSP is the collection of papers written by both undergraduate and graduate students in Michigan University. You can browse papers of your counterparts at 4 levels with 8 textual features, which are as follows:

- 4 levels: senior undergraduates, 1st year graduates, 2nd year graduates, and 3rd year graduates.

- 8 textual features: abstract, definitions, discussion of results, literature review, methodology section, problem-solution pattern, reference to sources, tables, graphs or figures.

5.5
The application of lexical knowledge

It's time to put theory into practice. In this part, you are required to read "This Week in *Science*" (including 17 abstracts) in the journal of *Science* and undertake three activities by applying the knowledge mentioned previously.

This Week in *Science*

(1) EVOLUTION

Locating myxomatosis resistance

Caroline Ash

Myxomatosis is a viral infection that was deliberately introduced from American cottontail rabbits into European rabbit populations to control their population. Over the past 60 years or so, similar resistance variants have emerged in parallel in the United Kingdom, France, and Australia. Alves et al. discovered that the basis for this resistance is polygenic, with selection converging on several host immunity and proviral alleles (see the Perspective by Miller and Metcalf). Interestingly, it now seems that the virus is counter-evolving immune suppressive traits.

(2) CAMBRIAN EXPLOSION

A treasure trove of Cambrian secrets

Sacha Vignieri

Animal life exploded in diversity and form during the Cambrian period about 500 million years ago. Fu et al. describe an early Cambrian fossil site in China that contains a variety of specimens, more than half of which are previously undescribed (see the Perspective by Daley). The site rivals previously described Cambrian sites, such as the Burgess Shale, and should help to elucidate biological innovation and diversification during this period.

(3) CANCER SIGNALING

Targeting a common eye cancer

John F. Foley

Uveal melanoma is a common cancer of the eye that frequently metastasizes. Most cases of uveal melanoma are driven by constitutively active mutants of the G protein α subunits $G\alpha_q$ and $G\alpha_{11}$; however, therapies that target signaling pathways downstream of these oncogenic drivers have been unsuccessful. Annala et al. confirmed that the plant-derived compound FR900359 directly inhibits oncogenic $G\alpha_{q/11}$ signaling in uveal melanoma cell lines in vitro. Furthermore, FR900359 reduced mutant $G\alpha_q$-driven uveal melanoma tumor growth in a mouse xenograft model.

(4) INORGANIC CHEMISTRY

Boron brings nitrogen together

Jake Yeston

Whereas carbon is prone to making chains, nitrogen usually sticks to itself just once in the particularly stable form of N_2. Légaré et al. now show that boron can coax two N_2 molecules together under reductive conditions below room temperature. Two borylene units sandwiched the resulting N_4 chain between them.

(5) OPTICS

Solving equations with waves

Ian S. Osborne

Signal processing of light waves can be used to represent certain mathematical functions and to perform computational tasks on signals or images in an analog fashion. Such processing typically requires complex systems of bulk optical elements such as lenses, filters, and mirrors. Mohammadi Estakhri et al. demonstrate that specially designed nanophotonic structures can take input waveforms encoded as complex mathematical functions, manipulate them, and provide an output that is the integral of the functions. The results, demonstrated for microwaves, provide a route to develop chip-based analog optical computers and computing elements.

(6) ATMOSPHERIC SCIENCE

Elucidating the sources of nightglow

Kollen Post

Even in the absence of light from the Sun and the stars, Earth's atmosphere emits its own glow. The sources of these glows vary, but nightglow has proven particularly enigmatic. Kalogerakis identified a mechanism that causes such glow in the mesosphere and lower thermosphere about 100 kilometers above Earth's surface. During the day, solar radiation breaks up oxygen and ozone, but by night, multiquantum vibrational-to-electronic energy transfer facilitates a similar process. The resultant individual oxygen atoms electrically excite surrounding molecules, producing nightglow.

(7) ION CHANNELS

Targeting sodium channels

Valda Vinson

Voltage-gated sodium (Na_v) channels have been implicated in cardiac and neurological disorders. There are many subtypes of these channels, making it challenging to develop specific therapeutics. A core α subunit is sufficient for voltage sensing and ion conductance, but function is modulated by β subunits and by natural toxins that can either act as pore blockers or gating modifiers (see the Perspective by Chowdhury and Chanda). Shen et al. present the structures of $Na_v1.7$ in complex with both $\beta1$ and $\beta2$ subunits and with animal toxins. Pan et al. present the structure of $Na_v1.2$ bound to $\beta2$ and a toxic peptide, the μ- conotoxin KIIIA. The structure shows why KIIIA is specific for $Na_v1.2$. These and other recently determined Na_v structures provide a framework for targeted drug development.

(8) INDUSTRIAL CHEMISTRY

Methane oxidation on the plus side

Jake Yeston

Industrial conversion of methane to alcohol derivatives involves a circuitous route that starts with overoxidation to carbon monoxide. More direct approaches in highly acidic media have shown promise at small scale but are not cost-effective. Díaz-Urrutia and Ott describe a reaction at pilot-plant scale that combines methane and sulfur trioxide directly in sulfuric acid to form methanesulfonic acid with no by-products (see the Perspective by Schüth). The reaction appears to proceed via a cationic chain mechanism initiated by a low concentration of added sulfonyl peroxide and propagated by CH_3^+.

(9) CANCER

A sweetener's not-so-sweet effects

Paula A. Kiberstis

Obesity increases an individual's risk of developing many types of cancer, including colorectal cancer. One of the factors driving the rise in obesity rates is thought to be the use of high-fructose corn syrup (HFCS) as a sweetener in soft drinks. Goncalves et al. found that ingestion of HFCS promotes the growth of intestinal cancer even in the absence of obesity in mouse tumor models. An enzyme in tumors (ketohexokinase) converts fructose to fructose-1- phosphate, which alters tumor cell metabolism and leads to enhanced cell growth. Whether a similar process occurs in humans remains to be seen.

(10) GEOPHYSICS

Automating geoscience analysis

Brent Grocholski

Solid Earth geoscience is a field that has very large set of observations, which are ideal for analysis with machine-learning methods. Bergen et al. review how these methods can be applied to solid Earth datasets. Adopting machine-learning techniques is important for extracting information and for understanding the increasing amount of complex data collected in the geosciences.

(11) ION CHANNELS

How activation leads to gating

Valda Vinson

Voltage-gated sodium (Na_v) channels are key players in electrical signaling. Central to their function is fast inactivation, and mutants that impede this cause conditions such as epilepsy and pain syndromes. The channels have four voltage-sensing domains (VSDs), with VSD4 playing an important role in fast inactivation. Clairfeuille et al. determined the structures of a chimera in which VSD4 of the cockroach channel Na_vPaS is replaced with VSD4 from human Na_v1.7, both in the apo state and bound to a scorpion toxin that impedes fast activation (see the

Perspective by Chowdhury and Chanda). The toxin traps VSD4 in a deactivated state. Comparison with the apo structure shows how interactions between VSD4 and the carboxyl-terminal region change as VSD4 activates and suggests how this would lead to fast inactivation.

(12) PLANT SCIENCE

Rapid response to tissue damage

Pamela J. Hines

　　Damaged plants are susceptible to microbial attack. In response to physical damage, plants proactively generate signal peptides to activate their immune systems. Hander et al. examined wound responses in the model plant *Arabidopsis thaliana*. They identified a metacaspase that releases an immunomodulatory signal peptide from its precursor form within 30 seconds of the damage. The metacaspase itself was activated by a burst of calcium released by tissue damage.

(13) EVOLUTION

Swarming in parallel toward sociality

Caroline Ash

　　The evolution of social behavior, and specifically of multicellularity, is poorly understood. An experimental model for multicellularity is the myxobacteria, which swarm and cooperate to form fruiting bodies in soil. Wielgoss et al. studied lineages of wild-caught myxobacteria. They found diversity, but also surprising genetic similarity, within fruiting bodies that was unlikely to be based on shared ancestry between them. Instead, reoccurrence of the same mutations seems to have occurred independently. These mutations have then been selected to confer similar phenotypes that converge on social behavior.

(14) GEOSCIENCE

Preparing for the next supereruption

Julia Fahrenkamp-Uppenbrink

　　The last volcanic supereruption—defined as having an eruption volume of more than 1,000 cubic kilometers—occurred about 27,000 years ago. In a Perspective, Papale and Marzocchi argue that if such an event were to occur today, it could pose an existential risk to humanity. Indeed, even a smaller eruption like that of Mount Tambora in the Lesser Sunda Islands, Indonesia, in 1815 has the potential to disrupt global economic activity. Although it is not possible to predict the eruption volume of individual volcanoes, statistical considerations suggest that the probability of a Mount Tambora-scale or larger eruption is sufficiently high to warrant the development of resilience plans for such an event.

(15) CANCER

Targeting RAS regulation

Gemma Alderton

The RAS signaling pathway controls cell survival and proliferation and is a possible target for cancer treatment. However, therapeutically targeting RAS is challenging. In a Perspective, Bivona discusses recent studies that identify upstream targets, the inhibition of which could suppress RAS signaling in cancer. Certain cancer-associated RAS pathway alterations leave RAS sensitive to regulation by signaling adaptors. Preclinical studies suggest that this regulation can be targeted to prevent RAS signaling and thus tumor progression.

(16) CANCER

Learning from one tumor to help another

Yevgeniya Nusinovich

Neuroendocrine prostate cancer is an aggressive tumor subtype that can arise late in the course of the disease and drive therapeutic resistance. Puca et al. tested an antibody-drug conjugate against delta-like protein 3 (DLL3), a recently identified therapeutic being tested in small cell lung cancer. DLL3 was present in most neuroendocrine prostate cancers, but not in localized tumors or normal prostate, and was associated with aggressive clinical features. Targeting DLL3 was effective in multiple mouse models as well as in a human patient.

(17) LYMPHOCYTE MIGRATION

Getting immune cells home

Anand Balasubramani

Immune cells are recruited to tissues from the lymphatic system via efferent lymphatics in response to insults ranging from skin allergies to flu infection. Immune cells recirculate back to draining lymph nodes by way of afferent lymphatics. Xiong et al. examined the role of sphingosine 1-phosphate (S1P) and its receptors (S1PRs) in the egress of T cells from tissues. Expression of S1PR1 and S1PR4 on T cells and engagement of S1PR2 on lymphatic endothelial cells were important for this process. Thus, S1PRs play a distinct role in the recirculation of immune cells back to the lymphatic system.

5.5.1 Activity 1: Spotting prefixes in research questions

Directions: Read the abstracts above and find the research questions according to the following steps.

- First, go over the topics in the passage and choose any four topics relevant to your majors in your group.

- Then, recall the structure of academic papers—IMRD, and attempt to spot the research questions in those abstracts.

- And then analyze the sentences and aims at prefixes meaning "opposite". For instance, according to the sentence "Fu et al. describe an early Cambrian fossil site in China that contains a variety of specimens, more than half of which are previously **undescribed** (see the Perspective by Daley)" in the second abstract, we can easily spot the word "**undescribed**", which means "something has not been described yet". Then we can tap into our vocabulary knowledge to inform us that this sentence indicates the research question. But in some abstracts, we cannot find any prefixes meaning "opposite". Alternatively, we may proceed to seek help from related words meaning "opposite".

- Eventually, translate those research questions and prepare for a presentation about the themes of those studies.

5.5.2 Activity 2: The revision box

Directions: You are given a vocabulary box by the teacher. This box mainly comprises of words from the abstracts above (verbs, adjectives, adverbs, etc.), most of which are from the Academic Word List. Change words chosen from the box into nouns, make sentences with these words and read the sentences in class following the steps below.

- The box with all the words is circulated around the class. You are required to pick a word which you will have to change into a noun first, and then construct a short and grammatical sentence. For instance, one adjective "viral" in the box is chosen from the sentence "Myxomatosis is a viral infection that was deliberately introduced from American cottontail rabbits into European rabbit populations to control their population" in the first abstract. Once you obtain the piece of paper with the word "viral", you must first change it into a noun (e.g. virus) and then you can construct a sentence with it.

- After 12 to 20 sentences, the sentences are analyzed to see if they are grammatically correct.

- Correction of the sentences can then be done and you are prompted to produce the correct sentences with the same word from the box if time permits.

5.5.3 Activity 3: Developing corpus skills

Directions: With COCA, you are required to fill in the following blanks with top ten common academic words with the prefixes, look up in the dictionary for their meanings and note down one of the sentences of these academic words relevant to your field from COCA.

Prefixes	Words	Meanings	Sentences
in-			
under-			

(Continued)

Prefixes	Words	Meanings	Sentences
dis-			
di-			

(Continued)

Prefixes	Words	Meanings	Sentences
electro-			
bio-			

(Continued)

Prefixes	Words	Meanings	Sentences
hydro-			
trans-			

(Continued)

Prefixes	Words	Meanings	Sentences
non-			
multi-			

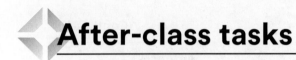

After-class tasks

❶ Consolidating quizzes

1. On COCA, you can do many kinds of searches of how words are used academically. On the website, click on "SECTIONS", choose "ACADEMIC", and then you can see your searches in academic genre. Write down the first sentence of the words or forms listed below.

"List":

(1) single words (e.g. consistent)

_____.

(2) phrases (e.g. in parallel)

_____.

(3) "fuzzy phrases" (e.g. more * than, * bit)

_____.

(4) wildcards (e.g. gen*)

_____.

5) synonyms (e.g. =beautiful, =gorgeous NOUN, =clever =man)

_____.

(6) customized word lists (e.g. @clothes, @colors @clothes)

_____.

"Collocates":

(1) single words (e.g. analysis)

_____.

(2) phrases (e.g. look into)

_____.

"Compare":

   (1) nouns that appear with *combine* and *incorporate*

       _____ .

   (2) adjectives with *risk* and *hazard*

       _____ .

   (3) nouns with *complex* and *complicated*

       _____ .

2. Spot those specialized terms in "This Week in *Science*" and find out how the authors paraphrased their meanings.

Abstracts	Specialized terms	Paraphrase	Chinese translation
1	myxomatosis		
3	uveal melanoma		
3	inhibit		
4	nitrogen		
5	optical		
6	glow		
7	therapeutics		
8	conversion		
11	impede		
12	wound response		
13	multicellularity		
14	supereruption		
15	proliferation		
16	tumor		
17	insult		

3. **Read the following passage and choose the best answer to each of the question that follows.**

Arid regions in the southwestern United States have become increasingly inviting playgrounds for the growing number of recreation seekers who own vehicles such as motorcycles or powered trail bikes and indulge in hill-climbing contests or in carving new trails in the desert. But recent scientific studies show that these off-road vehicles can cause damage to desert landscapes that has long-range effects on the area's water-conserving characteristics and on the entire ecology, both plant and animal. Research by scientists in the western Mojave Desert in California revealed that the compaction of the sandy arid soil resulting from the passage of one motorcycle markedly reduced the infiltration ability of the soil and created a stream runoff water that eroded the hillside surface. In addition, the researchers discovered that compaction caused by the off-road vehicles often killed native plant species and resulted in the invasion of different plant species within a few years. The native perennial species required many more years before they showed signs of returning. The scientists calculated that roughly a century would be required for the infiltration capacity of the Mojave soil to be restored after being compacted by vehicles.

(1) What is the main topic of the passage?
A. Problems caused by recreational vehicles.
B. Types of off-road vehicles.
C. Plants of the southwestern desert.
D. The increasing number of recreation seekers.

(2) According to the passage, what is being damaged?
A. Motorcycles.   B. The desert landscape.
C. Roads through the desert.   D. New plant species.

(3) According to the passage, the damage to plants is _____.
A. unnoticeable   B. superficial
C. long-lasting   D. irreparable

(4) According to the passage, what happens when the soil is compacted?
A. Little water seeps through.   B. Better roads are made.
C. Water is conserved.   D. Deserts are expanded.

(5) What is happening to the desert hillsides?
A. The topsoil is being eroded.
B. The surface is being irrigated.

C. There are fewer types of plants growing on them.

D. There are fewer streams running through them.

(6) According to the passage, what is happening to native plants in these areas?

A. They are becoming more compact.

B. They are adapting.

C. They are invading other areas.

D. They are dying.

4. Critical thinking: Do some research on some academicians in Chinese Academy of Sciences or Chinese Academy of Engineering in China. And reflect on what can attribute to their great accomplishments. Think about whether the spirit of artisans leads to their persistence in their research and contributions.

(Points for references: attributes; discernable; in the accomplished scientist or engineer; the route for the success; persistence; handicap; sufferings)

Ⅱ Mindmap

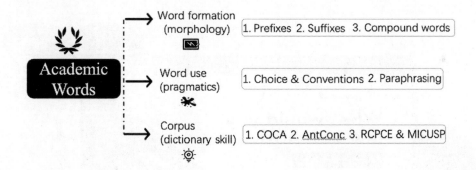

Ⅲ Project task

In this unit, you are expected to give a very brief oral introduction to the use of academic words. Choose one journal paper in your field and use the knowledge to analyze the papers on your own. You can record new words from the following perspectives:

- What type of prefixes are used most in research questions of those abstracts?

- What type of suffixes are used most?

- What compound words are used?
- What are the words you don't know and understand later by using paraphrasing?
- What are the collocations and synonyms of a new word you wish to record by using corpus?

Ⅳ Extended resources

1. **FutureLearn online course: English for Academic Study**

Brief information: FutureLearn offers you a powerful new way to learn online. Each course has been designed according to principles of effective learning, through storytelling, discussion, visible learning, and using community support to celebrate progress. If you are preparing to study at a university where the first language is English, this course aims to help you understand what is expected, develop skills to help you learn independently, and build your confidence.

You will have the opportunity to review the key vocabulary and concepts used in a university setting, and discover what tutors expect from students. You will also have the opportunity to practise skills to help you expand your vocabulary for an academic setting, including tools to help you pronounce new words.

2. **Further online resources: www. eapfoundation.com**

Brief information: The website provides you with a range of resources to boost your academic vocabulary learning. Among anything else, different vocabulary highlighters available are, in particular, helpful for you to know better how words in the Academic Word List are authentically used in your specific disciplines. Likewise, other sections, both writing and listening sections, are also well worth your time. Now you can download a journal paper in your discipline and attempt to learn how the 1,000 essential academic words are used.

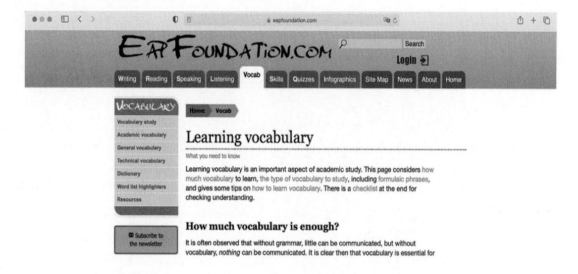

Unit 6

Grammar in Academic English

With the rapid development of science and technology, reading academic papers in English can help you understand the latest trends of disciplines quickly and accurately. And publishing English academic papers will also be a necessity if you want your voice to be heard in the academic world. Nevertheless, due to the lack of mastery of grammar in academic English, you may get puzzled during reading and your English academic papers may often be returned for revision and cannot get published after several attempts. The dilemma shows that although there is a common language core between general English and academic English, their expressions are not totally the same. In this unit, we will introduce the distinctive characteristics of grammar in academic English, like nominalization, verb tenses and voices, complex sentences, and comparative and superlative degrees. We will also introduce some grammar checking tools, in hope that they can help you when you read and write English academic papers.

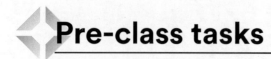

Pre-class tasks

❶ Suggested MOOC resources

You can scan the QR code to see if you are familiar with the grammatical characteristics of academic English and some grammar checking tools.

- Nominalization
- Numeral
- Comparative degree and superlative degree of adjectives and adverbs
- Grammar checking tools

❷ Pre-quizzes

1. Which of the following grammatical phenomena is NOT typical in academic English?

A. Present tense.

B. Nominalization.

C. First person pronouns.

D. The passive voice.

2. Which is the best form of the sentence "People's living standard has improved a lot" after nominalization?

A. The improving living standard.

B. People's living standard having improved a lot.

C. The improvement of people's living standard.

D. People's living standard being improved.

3. Which is the best form of the sentence "If you fail to arrive on time, your reservations will be canceled" after nominalization?

A. Your reservations will be canceled if failing to arrive on time.

B. Failing to arrive on time will cancel your reservations.

C. The cancellation of your reservations is because you fail to arrive on time.

D. Failure to arrive on time will result in the cancellation of your reservations.

4. Which of the following is the most appropriate to state the value of the research?

A. The research will help to understand deformation processes.

B. The research can help to understand deformation processes.

C. The research may help to understand deformation processes.

D. The research should help to understand deformation processes.

5. **Which of the following best fits in the blank?**

This method does not work _____ that one.

A. so well as

B. so best than

C. as better as

D. as better than

In-class tasks

6.1

General glimpse of grammar in academic English

In writing academic papers, knowing grammar well can help you write in the way that the academic world requires you to and play an important in publishing a paper. While grammar in academic English has a lot in common with that in general English, there are some typical grammatical characteristics worth us paying special attention to. Given that some of you may find it quite hard to grasp the grammatical characteristics of academic English and quite challenging to avoid grammar mistakes, at the very beginning of this unit, we will walk you through some typical grammatical characteristics of academic English and hope that you will find it helpful for your academic reading and writing.

6.1.1 Higher frequency of using nominalization

Different from general English, nominalization is widely used in academic English writing and considered to be one of the typical grammatical characteristics of academic English. The reason is that academic English is usually more refined, formal and abstract, and the use of nominalization can achieve the effect. Compare the following two sentences and try to find where nominalization is adopted.

- As water vapor pressure increases, more gold is **solubilized**.
- Gold **solubility** increases with increasing water vapor pressure.

As is seen clearly from the sentences above, "solubilized" is nominalized into "solubility" in the second sentence, which changes the first complex sentence into a simple one.

6.1.2 Higher frequency of using the present tense

Compared with general English, academic English has a comparatively lower frequency of using the past tense but a higher frequency of using the present tense. This is because academic English is generally used to discuss general truths or facts that do not involve the concept of time. In time and adverbial clauses, we can also use the present tense to describe actions that will happen in the future or will happen according to plans or scientific laws. Nevertheless, the past tense is mainly used to describe the work done in the past, so it is relatively seldom used.

6.1.3 Long and complex sentences

In academic English, sentences have more complicated structures and are much longer, conveying more information. The long and complex sentences are usually formed by connectives and various kinds of subordinate clauses. Therefore, when writing academic papers, you should not only be able to analyze and identify the sentence structures correctly in order to grasp their meaning, but also be capable of producing long and complex sentences yourself. See the following sentence and try to find its main structure.

The hypothesis that magmatic vapors play a major role in the transport of base and precious metals to sites of ore deposition first gained credence in the modern era through the pioneering study of Henley and Mcnabb, and subsequently found many new advocates who were persuaded by the results of fluid inclusion and experimental studies.

The sentence above is quite long and complex, excerpted from an academic paper, and its main structure is: The hypothesis first gained credence and subsequently found many new advocates.

6.1.4 Higher frequency of using the passive voice

Academic English is highly objective and abstract, and the meanings of expressions are extremely clear. In order to avoid the interference of human factors and the fuzziness of expressions, various pronouns are generally not preferred, and the passive voice is often used so as to omit the agent and depersonalize the information. The following excerpt is the introduction of the experimental method, adopting the past tense, and the passive voice is used to omit the agent and show the objectivity of the experiment.

> The experiments **were conducted** in batch-type titanium grade 2 autoclaves at temperatures between 300 ℃ and 450 ℃ using a similar experimental method to that of previous studies. Autoclaves **were heated** in a Barnstead Thermolyne muffle furnace equipped with a stainless steel box to reduce thermal gradients. The temperature **was recorded** with an Omega temperature logger using a K-thermocouple and **was maintained** to within 0.5 ℃ of the desired experimental temperature. Prior to the experiments, the autoclaves **were heated** to 450 ℃, thereby producing a protective TiO_2 layer, which is inert at the experimental conditions. The volume of each autoclave **was determined** by filling the autoclave with distilled water from a Teflon flask, and weighing the autoclave before and after filling to an accuracy of ± 0.1 g. (Hurtig & William-Jones, 2014)

6.1.5 Few abbreviations and omissions

Academic English writing is formal and rigorous, so it is quite natural to use less abbreviations and omissions. For example, it is better to use "it is" instead of "it's", and "that" as an object clause marker is seldom omitted in academic English. Look at the following example:

> As reported above, our experimental data indicate **that** the gold monochloride monomer is the dominant gold species in low density H_2O at temperatures up to 450 ℃.
>
> From the modelling, **it is** evident that the dimers predominate over a wide range of Cl_2 pressures and temperatures, and are only replaced by their monomers as dominant species at very low Cl_2 pressures and correspondingly low gold fugacity. (Hurtig & William-Jones, 2014)

In this part, we have briefly introduced the grammatical characteristics of academic English. Next, we will elaborate on these features.

6.2
Nominalization

Nominalization refers to the grammatical process in which verbs or adjectives are converted into nouns in certain ways, such as adding suffixes and transformation. And it has several functions.

6.2.1 Functions of nominalization

6.2.1.1 Compactness

Nominalization can transform a simple sentence into a noun phrase and a complex sentence into a simple sentence, while the meaning of the sentence remains basically unchanged. In this way, the information originally distributed in several sentences is compressed into a single sentence by nominalization, thus increasing the sentence complexity. Look at the following example to see how the information is compacted.

- The driver **drove** the bus too rapidly down the hill, so the brakes **failed**. → The driver's over-rapid downhill **driving** of the bus resulted in brake **failure**.

6.2.1.2 Objectivity

Nominalization can make the subject of a sentence omitted, and the sentence only objectively describes the existing facts, and does not directly involve the actor.

- We can **improve** its performance when we use superheated steam. → An **improvement** of its performance can be effected by the use of superheated steam.

In this case, after omitting the subject "we" in the first sentence by nominalization, the second sentence only states facts, thus becoming more objective.

6.2.1.3 Formality

Use of nominalization is one important marker of academic English and can make the language more formal. Now compare the following two sentences and try to figure out which is more formal.

- If the item is **exposed** for long, it will rapidly **deteriorate**.
- Prolonged **exposure** will result in rapid **deterioration** of the item.

Obviously, the second one is more formal.

6.2.1.4 Cohesion

If the verbs or adjectives mentioned in the former sentences are mentioned again in the following text, we can use their noun forms to play a connecting role.

And once the material is fully **solidified**, the history of this dendritic **solidification** remains imprinted with the material, with variations in composition observed in numerous locations.

In this sentence, the corresponding noun form of the action verb "solidify" mentioned in the subordinate sentence is used in the main clause, which makes the sentence more logical and natural.

Now that we know the importance of nominalization, how can we realize it? Next we will look at nominalization at different levels.

6.2.2 Nominalization at different levels

6.2.2.1 Nominalization at lexical level

At the lexical level, nominalization mainly involves the change of part of speech, which is usually achieved by adding suffixes to a word. This is the first step of nominalization.

In-class exercise 1:

Directions: Add suffixes to the words given below to form nouns.

Given words	Suffixes added	Nouns formed
develop		
prepare		
protect		

(Continued)

Given words	Suffixes added	Nouns formed
classify		
erode		
stable		
popular		
flexible		
original		
efficient		

6.2.2.2 Nominalization at phrasal level

With the nominalization at the lexical level, some changes will first take place at the phrasal level, thus leading to different phrasal expressions. Please note that "NOUN" in the following subtitles refers to the nominalized nouns.

1. NOUN + of + Noun

- The temperature **varies**. → the **variation** of the temperature
- People **separate** aluminum. → the **separation** of aluminum
- The system is **unstable**. → the **instability** of the system

2. NOUN + of + Noun + Preposition + Noun

- The planets **move** around the sun. → the **motion**s of the planets around the sun
- Einstein **formulated** the theory. → the **formulation** of the theory by Einstein
- Radar is **superior** to ordinary vision. → the **superiority** of radar to ordinary vision

3. Preposition + NOUN

- Before the seed **germinates**, it is watered. → Before **germination**, the seed is watered.

4. Other forms of nominalization

- lay **emphasis** on, attach **importance** to
- I have a **doubt** whether the news is true.
- power **generation**, hail **prevention**

These forms of nominalization have already become fixed patterns.

6.2.2.3 Nominalization at syntactic level

After changing a simple sentence into a phrasal expression, you can turn a compound or complex sentence into a simple one by connecting the two phrasal expressions with verbs or phrases like "cause", "arise from", "lead to", "result in", "effect", "prove", "be", "bring about", "need", "remain", "seem", "appear", etc. Which verb should be used depends on the logical relationship between the two phrasal expressions. Look at the examples below to see how the verb has been chosen.

- WeChat is very **popular**, and it makes people's life more **convenient**. → The **popularity** of WeChat *brings* more **convenience** to people's life.
- The driver **drove** the bus too rapidly down the hill, so the brakes **failed**. → The driver's overrapid downhill **driving** of the bus *resulted in* brake **failure**.
- If the item is **exposed** for long, it will rapidly **deteriorate**. → Prolonged **exposure** will *result in* rapid **deterioration** of the item.

In-class exercise 2:

Directions: *Change the following underlined sentences into phrases using nominalization.*

(1) If children frequently contact their parents, they will get more emotional support.

_____ brings about more emotional support for them.

(2) The company has developed the technology for elderly care facilities and it can provide much more convenience for empty nesters in daily activities.

_____ can provide much more convenience for empty nesters in daily activities.

In-class exercise 3:

Directions: *Rewrite the following sentences using nominalization.*

(1) If you fail the exam, you will be expelled from the school.

_____

(2) Another acquaintance confessed that he is constantly yearning for a new electronic gadget.

_____

6.3
Verb tenses and voices

When writing an experimental research report, you may find it quite difficult to use verb tenses appropriately. To solve this problem, we will look at the use of verb tenses and voices in different parts of an experimental report. A typical experimental research report consists of five parts: abstract, introduction, method, results, and discussion. Given that abstract is the last part of the report to be written, let's start from the introduction instead.

6.3.1 Introduction

The introduction serves as an orientation for readers of the report, giving them the perspective they need to understand the detailed information coming in later sections. Generally, it can be divided into five elements: the setting, the literature review, the gap, the purpose, and the value.

Table 6-1   Verb tenses used in the introduction section

Information	Verb tenses mainly used
1. the setting	present or present perfect tense
2. the literature review	present or past or present perfect tense
3. the gap	present or present perfect tense
4. the purpose	past or present or future tense
5. the value	modal auxiliaries

The first element provides the readers with the background knowledge necessary to see the particular topic of your research in relation to a general area of study. The present tense and the present perfect tense are usually used in this part.

In the second element of literature review, you need to cite the work of other authors, so we will mainly look at the verb tenses in the citations. Generally speaking, your choices of verb tenses in citations are usually decided by the different focus either on the information provided by that author or on the author himself, so there are mainly two forms of citations.

In the first form, the sentence focuses on the information provided by the author, while the author's name and date of publication are parenthetically attached at the end of the sentence. In such cases, the present tense is often used. In the second form, the author's name serves as the subject of the sentence, followed by the date or citation number in parentheses and then by the information. In these citations, the simple past tense is usually adopted. Besides, please note that when the information is about the research area of several authors, the present perfect tense is often used.

After the literature review comes the third element. Here you need to point out a gap, that is, an important research area not investigated by other authors. And you can use the present tense or the present perfect tense to indicate the gap.

In element 4, the statement of purpose can be written from either research or a report orientation. If you choose the research orientation, you should use the past tense, because the research activity has already been completed; if you choose to use the report orientation, use the present or future tense.

Element 5, the statement of value, is usually written in a way that suggests an attitude of tentativeness or modesty on the part of the author. You should not be too sure of the benefits of your work, either practical or theoretical. This is accomplished by using modal auxiliaries. Yet selecting the most appropriate modal auxiliary is often a problem because the meanings of some of these words differ only slightly from one another. Here is a summary of the modal auxiliaries you often use in elements 4 and 5, and the degree of tentativeness of these words is from sure to tentative.

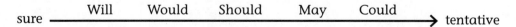

sure ——— Will   Would   Should   May   Could ——→ tentative

In order to better understand the function of each element, let us briefly look at all five elements of an introduction. The following is the introduction to the research report about computers in education and please note the verb tenses used in each element.

Element 1
During the past 40 years, the United States has experienced the integration of the computer into society. Progress has been made to the point that small, inexpensive computers with expanded capabilities are available for innumerable uses. Many schools have purchased and are purchasing microcomputers for infusion into their directed learning programs.

Element 2
Most individuals seem to agree that the microcomputer will continue to hold an important role in education. Gubser (1980) and Hinton (1980) suggested phenomenal increases in the numbers of computers both in the school and the home in the near future. Schmidt (1982) identified three types of microcomputer use in classrooms: the object of a course, a support tool, and a means of providing instruction. Foster and Kleene (1982) cite four uses of Stage II microcomputers in vocational agriculture: drill and practice, tutorial, simulation and problem solving. The findings of studies examining the use of various forms of computer-assisted instruction (CAI) have been mixed. Studies by Hickey (1968) and Honeycutt (1974) indicated superior results with CAI while studies by Ellis (1978), Caldwell (1980) and Belzer (1976) indicated little or no significant effect.

Element 3
Although much work has been done to date, more studies need to be conducted to ascertain the effects of microcomputer-assisted instruction in teaching various subjects in a variety of learning situations.

Element 4
The purpose of this study was to ascertain the effect of using microcomputer-assisted instruction as compared to a lecture-discussion technique in teaching principles and methods of cost recovery and investment credit on agricultural assets to graduate students in agricultural education.

Element 5
This topic was identified as being of importance to teachers in providing them the necessary background to teach lessons in farm records. (Rohrbach & Stewart, 1986)

In-class exercise 4:

Directions: *Fill in the table below according to the introduction above.*

Information elements	Verb tenses mainly used
1. the setting	
2. the literature review	
3. the gap	
4. the purpose	
5. the value	

6.3.2 Methods

The method section is useful for readers who want to know how the methodology of your study may have influenced your results, or who are interested in replicating or extending your study. We'll only focus on two main parts of the method section— procedures and materials.

Procedures you used in carrying out your study should be described in the simple past tense. Sentences that are not written in the past tense usually describe standard procedures that are commonly used by others. Either the active or the passive voice can be used when you describe the procedure in your report. However, the passive voice is conventionally used in order to depersonalize the information. In other words, you can omit the agent, placing the emphasis on the procedure and how it was done.

Materials often refer to the items used in the study. When describing samples used in a study, we commonly use the past tense. However, if the equipment used in your study is standard or conventional in your field and probably familiar to most other researchers, you should describe it with the present tense. The similar convention also applies to the description of other materials. Both the active voice and the passive voice can be used in this part. The passive voice is used when a human agent is manipulating the materials or to describe an action involving a nonhuman agent. Besides, you should also notice that when the materials operate by themselves, the active voice is usually used.

6.3.3 Results

The results section presents the findings of the study in both figures and written text. Here we focus on the text, which usually consists of three main Functions—location of the figure, report of the findings and comment on the findings.

Table 6-2 Verb tenses used in the results section

Information elements	Verb tenses mainly used
1. Location of the figure	present tense
2. Report of the findings	past tense
3. Comment on the findings	present tense or modal auxiliaries or tentative verbs like "suggest"

When commenting on the findings, please note that: if you compare your results with the results of other studies, use the present tense; if you give a possible explanation for the results, use a modal auxiliary; if you generalize from the results, use "may". Besides, you can also use tentative verbs in the present tense instead of modal auxiliaries to generalize from results.

> The solubility of gold **was** measured in HCl-bearing aqueous vapors buffered by Mo-oxides at temperatures between 300 ℃ and 450 ℃ (Figures 3 and 4). Results of these experiments **are** presented in Appendices A2.1–A2.5. Gold concentrations **ranged** between 0.9 ppb in condensates from the low-density vapors to 4.6 ppm in condensates from the intermediate density fluids. The former **corresponds** to a HCl fugacity of 0.012 bar in experiments conducted at 300 ℃ and the latter to a HCl fugacity of 0.037 bar in experiments conducted at 400 ℃. At each temperature, i.e., 300, 340, 367, 400 and 450 ℃, two sets of experiments **were** conducted. (Hurtig & William-Jones, 2014)

6.3.4 Discussion

Discussion, sometimes called "conclusion", is the last major section of the report, followed by the list of references. In this section, you step back and take a broader look at your findings and your study as a whole and examine your work in the larger context of your field. Usually there are six information elements in this section.

Table 6-3　Verb tenses used in Discussion

Information elements	Verb tenses mainly used
1. Purpose or hypothesis	past or present perfect tense
2. Review of the findings	
3. Explanations or speculations	past or present tense or modal auxiliaries
4. Limitations	
5. Implications of the study	present tense or modal auxiliaries or tentative verbs like "suggest"
6. Recommendations for future research and practical applications	

Please look at the following example and notice what verb tenses are used.

The CCWT **is** a well-known theory extensively used in compressional tectonic, but **has not previously been applied** to rifted continental margins. However, the three fundamental requirements of CCWT **are** valid for hyper-extended continental crust in the most distal parts of magma-poor rifted margins. The purpose of this study **is** to measure the crustal wedge aperture angles ($\alpha+\beta$) at a set of hyper-extended continental margins, to test the applicability of CCWT and to determine whether CCWT **can resolve** the final geometries of crustal wedges at hyper-extended continental margins. It **is** important to note that this theory **is** only applicable for the last deformation continental phase and **affects** only the frictional hyper-extended crust, prior ductile and brittle deformation are out of the scope of this study. (Nirrengarten et al., 2016)

Although not all the elements will be included in every report, most writers will follow the specific-to-general movement. The information elements that are commonly included refer most directly to the study and its findings. They include the first four information elements. Then the writer focuses more generally on the importance of the study for other researchers.

6.3.5 Abstract

Abstracts from almost all fields of study are written in a very similar way and the typical information sequence of an abstract is background information, the purpose or principal activity of the study, methods, results and finally conclusion. The verb tenses used in the abstract are directly related to those you used in the corresponding sections mentioned earlier.

Table 6-4   Verb tenses used in the abstract section

Information elements	Verb tenses mainly used
1. Background information	past or present perfect tense
2. Purpose or principal activity	present or future tense
3. Methods	past or present perfect tense
4. Results	present tense
5. Conclusion	present tense or modal auxiliaries or verbs like "suggest"

Look at the following example to get a general idea about what verb tenses are used in an abstract.

Gold solubility and speciation in low density H_2O–HCl vapor **were** investigated experimentally at temperatures between 300 ℃ and 450 ℃, and pressures up to 366 bar using batch-type titanium autoclaves. Concentrations of total dissolved gold in the experimental condensates **ranged** from 0.9 ppb at 300 ℃ and 48 bar to 4.6 ppm at 400 ℃ and 297 bar. The hydrated gold monochloride species (AuCl $(H_2O)_y$) **is** the dominant gold species under the experimental conditions. Gold solubility **increases** with increasing water vapor pressure and **can** be expressed by the reaction,

$$Au_s + xHCl_g + yH_2O_g = AuCl_x(H_2O)_y + x/2H_{2,g} \ K_{s,y}$$

The hydration number (y) **increases** with increasing pressure, thereby indicating that solvation by H_2O molecules in the gas-phase is analogous to that in liquid-like fluids. Results of extrapolation of the data using a linear relationship of logKs, y with reciprocal temperature **compare** well with published experimental data for the solubility of gold at 1,000 ℃ in dilute HCl-bearing water vapor. At high water vapor pressure, the solubility of gold in an aqueous vapor with an HCl fugacity of 0.1 bar **is** similar to that in a vapor with approximately 50 bar H_2S, in which AuS is the dominant gaseous gold species. This **indicates** that hydrated gold monochloride species **may** play an important role in magmatic-hydrothermal systems dominated by low density aqueous fluids with high HCl concentrations. Modelling of the cooling and decompression of HCl-bearing intermediate-density (0.35 g cm^{-3}) aqueous fluids **shows** that gold solubility reaches a maximum of 253 ppm at 500 ℃. In fluids with densities of 0.20 and 0.10 g cm^{-3} the corresponding solubility maxima **are** reached at ~ 400 ℃, and **are** of 14.8 and 0.49 ppm, respectively. (Hurtig & William-Jones, 2014)

Through the examples above, you may have noticed that the verb tenses listed in the tables are not totally correspondent with the examples given. Actually, this part just gives you a broad picture of which verb tense should be used. When it comes to reading or writing a specific English academic research paper, please note that there may be some minor changes or differences concerning the parts included in a specific research paper or the use of verb tenses and voices in each part. So remember to do some research under the specific context before writing the actual research paper.

6.4
Complex sentences

In academic English, whether in reading literature or writing, you will see a lot of complex sentences. Use of complex sentences is also one of the typical grammatical characteristics of academic English. However, most students will find it a big problem to produce complex sentences instead of simple ones. In this part, we are going to introduce five methods you can use to revise simple sentences, making them more complex and sophisticated.

6.4.1　Add a second (or more) complete sentence

When you add a second complete sentence to a simple sentence, the result is a compound sentence. It is used to give equal weight to two closely related ideas. The two complete statements in a compound sentence are usually connected by a comma and a coordinating word like "and", "but", "for", "or", "nor", "so", and "yet". Here are two examples, in which each sentence contains two ideas that the writer considers equal in importance.

- A transformer cannot be called a machine **for** it has no moving parts.

- The broken bolt was fixed during lunchtime, **and** the bus ran smoothly for the news cameras.

6.4.2 Add a dependent clause

When you add a dependent clause to a simple sentence, the result is a complex sentence. A dependent clause begins with one of the following subordinating words:

after	if, even if	when, whenever
although, though	in order that	where, wherever
as	since	whether
because	that, so that	which, whichever
before	unless	while
even though	until	who
how	what, whatever	whose

A complex sentence is used to emphasize one idea over another. The important idea is expressed as an independent clause, while the less important one is subordinate to the independent clause, starting with the subordinating words. Let's see some examples below.

- **If** air is matter, it must act like other matters.
- Heat is developed **whenever** friction forces are present.
- There is every possibility **that** this newly designed elevator will pass the safety test.

Except compound sentences and complex sentences, much more complicated sentences can be formed when a second independent clause is added to a complex sentence, or a dependent clause is subordinate to a compound sentence. Look at the following examples.

- Applications of the fuel cell may seem futuristic, **but** the device itself dates from 1839, **when** the Welsh-born British jurist and scientist Sir William Robert Groves devised "gas battery".
- The circuit consisted of a lead (a sensor) connected to the rim of the cup, an LED **that** lit up **when** the circuit was closed, and a conducting fluid in the cup, **which** closed the circuit **when** it reached the rim.

6.4.3 Begin with a special opening word or phrase

Among the special openers that can be used to start sentences are *-ed* words, *-ing* words, *-ly* words, **to** word groups, and prepositional phrases. Here are examples of all five kinds of openers:

- **Looked** at in another way, it is impossible for a single force to produce the same effect as a couple.
- **Designed** primarily for protons, this accelerator has achieved energies of 300 GeV.
- **Being** heated, magnetized steel will lose its magnetism.
- **Flowing** through a circuit, the current will lose part of its energy.
- **Similarly**, an electric charge produces an electric field around it.
- **To** do this, it is necessary to decide the type of lamination to be used.
- **To** understand and use physics, we must have a knowledge of basic mathematics.
- **To every action** there must be an equal and opposite reaction.
- **For instance**, we might think of the hypothalamus as a thermostat.

6.4.4 Place adjectives or verbs in a series

Various parts of a sentence may be placed in a series. Among these parts are adjectives and verbs. Here are examples of both in a series.

- Almost all the **residential**, **commercial** and **industrial** current in the world today is alternating current.
- A cart of mass m is stationary on a perfectly **smooth**, **frictionless**, **horizontal** path.
- If you are walking with a cup of liquid, **focus** on it and **adjust** your motion if you see it is about to spill.

6.4.5 Running dictation activity

Directions: Work in small teams and play different roles of runners and writers. When the game begins, one of your team members runs to read and memorize the sentence pasted on the wall, and then runs back and quietly dictates what he remembered to the writer in the team. Over several turns your team will write down the whole sentence. The winner is the team that finishes the sentence first without any mistakes. The following are some sentences that can be used.

(1) Some people claim that hackers are good guys who simply push the

boundaries of knowledge without doing any harm (at least not on purpose), whereas "crackers" are the real bad guys.

(2) This can refer to gaining access to the stored contents of a computer system, gaining access to the processing capabilities of a system, or capturing information being communicated between systems.

(3) Unknown vulnerabilities, which the owner or operator of a system is not aware of, may be the result of poor engineering, or may arise from unintended consequences of some of the needed capabilities.

(4) Another type of attack is one that is preprogrammed against specific vulnerabilities and is launched without any specific target—it is blasted out shotgun style with the goal of reaching as many potential targets as possible.

(5) Also, consider getting a hardware firewall and limiting the flow of data to and from the Internet to only the few select ports you actually need, such as e-mail and Web traffic.

6.5
Comparative degree and superlative degree

When presenting the results of your experiment, you probably need to compare the data or studies, so it is not avoidable to adopt the comparative and superlative degrees. Given that some of you may still have difficulty using the comparative and superlative degrees flexibly, in this part we are going to elaborate on their uses. This part covers three key points, namely, different forms of comparative and superlative degrees, sentence patterns, and specific uses.

6.5.1 Different forms of comparative and superlative degrees

First let us take a look at the grammar rules of comparative and superlative degrees for adjectives and adverbs. The constitution of comparative and superlative degrees can be divided into regular forms and irregular forms. Most comparative and superlative adjectives and adverbs are regular forms, and only a few are irregular forms.

There are two ways of expressing regular forms. One way is to add "-er" and "-est" to the original words. The other is to add "more" or "most" before the original words. Generally speaking, monosyllables adopt the former way, such as "fast", "faster", "fastest", while the adjectives or adverbs with three or more syllables usually adopt the latter, such as "instructive", "more instructive", "most instructive". Disyllables can adopt both ways, such as "clever", "cleverer / more clever", "cleverest / most clever". Besides, please pay special attention to the spelling of the adjectives ending with "e", stressed closed syllable words, and those ending with "consonant + y". Please see the table below for reference.

Table 6-5　Regular forms of the comparative and superlative degrees

Constitution		Original	Comparative	Superlative
monosyllables and some disyllables	Add "-er/-est"	fast	faster	fastest
	Add "-r/-st" to adjectives ending with the letter "e"	large	larger	largest
	For stressed closed syllable words, double the consonant and then add "-er/-est"	big	bigger	biggest
	For disyllables ending with "consonant + y", change "y" into "i", then add "-er/-est"	early	earlier	earliest
polysyllabic words and some disyllables	Add "more/most"	instructive	more instructive	most instructive

There are a few adjectives and adverbs whose comparative and superlative forms are irregular. So you need to pay special attention and memorize them.

Table 6-6　Irregular forms of the comparative and superlative degrees

Original	Comparative	Superlative
good/well	better	best
bad/badly	worse	worst

(Continued)

Original	Comparative	Superlative
many/much	more	most
little	less	least
far	farther (further)	farthest (furthest)

6.5.2 Sentence patterns

6.5.2.1 Sentence patterns of the comparative degree

Next, let us take a look at how the comparative adjectives and adverbs are used in a sentence. You can also use it as a review of sentence structures of the comparative degree.

1. **adj./adv. (comparative) + than + compared subject (+ is, are, was, were, do, does, etc.)**

- In carbon dioxide, the velocity of sound is **slower than** it is in air.
- Positive ions contain **fewer** electrons **than** protons.
- An object at the top of a mountain will weigh **less** there **than** it does at sea level.

What's worth noting here is that "than + compared object" can be omitted sometimes. And words like "is", "are", "do", "does" are usually omitted as well, but can be used after or before the compared subject for the sake of emphasis.

- Liquids transmit sound more rapidly than **gases (do)**.

Besides, when comparison is made between two objects, there can be some modifiers before the comparative words. Here are different adverbs of degree that can be used as modifiers: "much", "far", "very much", "well", "a lot", "a great deal", "considerably", "greatly", "enormously", "significantly", "substantially", "appreciably", "incredibly", "immeasurably", "noticeably", etc.

- Sound travels **much more rapidly** in hydrogen than in air.
- Stiffness is a **far more effective** factor in controlling the velocity of sound waves than is density.

What's more, comparative degree can be modified by "N times".

- Alpha particles weigh about **four times more** than neutrons.
- The electrostatic force is 2.3×10^{39} **times stronger** than the gravitational force.

2. Sentence patterns indicating a continuously changing process

Some sentence patterns can be used to show continuous change, like "adj./adv. (comparative) + and + adj./adv. (comparative)", "ever + adj./adv. (comparative)", "more and more + adj./adv. (original)", and "increasingly+ adj./adv. (original)".

- Electronic devices are becoming **smaller and smaller**, but **more and more complicated**.
- Electronics industry is producing **ever more precise** instruments.
- Large computers have become **increasingly complex**.

3. the + adj./adv. (comparative)..., the + adj./adv. (comparative)

We can divide this structure into two parts. The former part is the conditional sentence part, which can only use the simple present tense. However, the latter part is the subject part which can use the simple present tense or the simple future tense. Besides, when the predicate of any part above is "linking verb + predicative", "be" can be omitted in large part. But when the subject is pronoun, "be" cannot be omitted. What's more, when the comparative degree of adjectives is used as the attribute of the object in a sentence, the object must be moved to the beginning of the sentence together with the comparative adjective.

- **The bigger** the slope, **the faster** the graph rises.
- **The smaller** the wire, **the more** resistance you have.

4. as + adj./adv. (original) + as + compared subject (+ is, are, was, were, do, does, etc.)

The structure can be understood as "the same as" and take the following sentence as an example.

- Radio waves travel **as fast as** light (does).

If we want to stress the mood, "as light does" can be replaced by "as does light". The negative form of the structure is "A is not as/so + original degree + as +

compared subject B", which means A is inferior to B. See the following examples for reference.

- Tin does **not** have **as hig**h a melting point **as** lead (does).
- The melting point of Tin is **not so high as** lead.

6.5.2.2 Sentence patterns of the superlative degree

The final sentence pattern is the expression of superlative, "(the) + superlative + comparison range". If the comparison happens among three or four objects, superlative should be used. Putting the brackets on definite article "the" means we don't have to add "the" before superlative adverbs. So we can see from the following examples there is often a comparison range to express superlative meaning. Usually, the comparison range is placed before or after a sentence, and sometimes can be omitted. There are three ways to express comparison range which are "of + phrase", "in + phrase" and "among + phrase". We should notice that each singular or plural noun in prepositional phrases is different. Besides, in modern English, "among" can usually be replaced by "of".

- **Of all the functions** encountered in electrical engineering, perhaps **the most important** one is the sinusoid.
- The pressure in the liquid is **least** where the speed is **greatest**.
- The planet **nearest** the sun is Mercury.
- Figure 2-1 shows **the most familiar** type of lever.

6.5.3 Specific uses in academic paper

After learning the different forms and sentence patterns of the comparative and superlative degrees, we will see how they are used in English academic papers. Generally speaking, the comparative structure can often be used to compare the experiment data, state the consequence, or contrast the experiment objects.

6.5.3.1 Comparison of two or more sets of data

The following are some common expressions:

- sb. tends to perform better/worse in tests of X than sb.
- sb. tends to have greater/less...

- sb. makes more/fewer errors in tests of X
- One of the most crucial/striking/marked/salient/notable/obvious/significant/ prominent/noticeable/surprising/fundamental/widely-reported differences between X and Y is...

6.5.3.2 Comparison of two or more groups of subjects

The following are some common expressions:

- As shown in Figure 1,
- Looking at Figure 3, it is apparent that
- As can be seen from the table (above),
- From the graph above we can see that
- It can be seen from the data in Table 1 that

the X group reported significantly more Y than the other two groups.

See the excerpt from the result part of an academic paper, and find how the comparative or superlative degrees are used.

The gold fugacity in graphite-buffered (log fo_2 = −28.44 at 367 ℃) experiments was approximately two orders of magnitude **lower** at 367 ℃ than the gold fugacity measured in Mo-oxide-buffered experiments (Figure 4c). This result too is supported by extrapolations based on $logK_{s,y}$ values determined from MoO_2–MoO_3 buffered experiments (Figure 4c, dark solid line). It therefore follows that the thermodynamic properties obtained from Mo-buffered experiments can be reliably applied to a large range of fo_2 conditions. At 300 ℃, graphite is inert and does not buffer the gas-phase. Consequently, the gold concentrations in the experimental condensates at this temperature were **higher** even than those measured in condensates from the MoO_2–MoO_3 buffered experiments at the same temperature (Fig. 4a). (Hurtig & William-Jones, 2014)

6.5.3.3 Comparison in conclusions or suggestions

In the parts of suggestions or conclusions, we can also use the comparative and superlative degrees to put forward the features of the research, or make a contrast with predecessors of their findings and innovations, or give a piece of advice or enlightenment to other research.

The study						
The findings	would/					adopted...
Smith's paper	might	more...		the author		used..
The conclusions	have	far more...	if	the research	had	included...
The questionnaire	been	much more...		he/she		provided...
The research						considered...
						focused on...

The following is an excerpt from the discussion part of the same academic paper by Hurtig and Williams-Jones (2014). Read it quickly and find how the comparative or superlative degrees are used.

At water vapor pressure below 150 bar, the gold fugacity in the system HCl–H_2O is one to two orders of magnitude **lower** than in the H_2S–H_2O system (Figure 10a). As in the study of Archibald et al. (2001), Zezin et al. (2011) modelled their data assuming a linear increase in gold fugacity with increasing log f_{H_2O}. We have fitted their data to an exponential function (which only became apparent after normalization of the gold fugacity to H_2S fugacity) and, as is evident from Figures 10b and c, the profiles for the fugacity of the AuS species as a function of log f_{H_2O} are very similar to those for AuCl. The solvation shells of both species are dominated by water molecules with only one potential H_2S molecule participating in the solvation of $AuS(H_2S)_{y-1}(H_2O)_x$ in H_2O–H_2S gas mixtures. Comparison of the two sets of profiles reveals that the solvated AuS species is **more volatile** and that the dependence of hydration on density is **less pronounced** than for the hydrated AuCl species. This can be explained by the observation that the relativistic bond stabilization is dependent on the ligand electronegativity, and that AuCl has a **smaller** dipole moment and will experience **greater** destabilization than AuS. (Hurtig & William-Jones, 2014)

In this part, we learned the different forms of the comparative and superlative degrees of adjectives and adverbs, summarized the common sentence patterns, and specific ways to use them in an academic paper. We should not only get familiar with them, but also understand their flexible and practical application in the real literature. Only if we combine the grammar rules into the practical usage can we achieve and master the essence.

6.6
Grammar checking tools

When you finish your first draft, it's time for you to revise and polish it. Then grammar checking is a must, but how to do grammar checking effectively? One ideal way is to ask some English native speakers to help you, but it may not be so easy to find the right one. Mostly, you have to check the grammar of your paper again and again all by yourself. So how to do grammar checking effectively is really a big challenge. In this part, some tools are recommended to help you to do grammar checking.

6.6.1 Grammarly

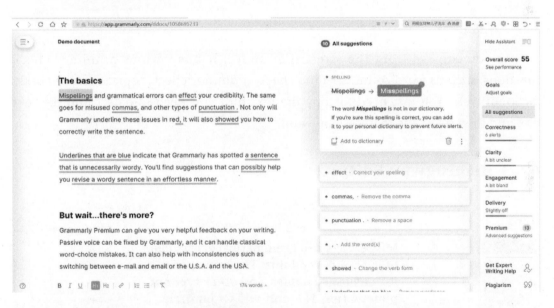

This is a grammar checking application developed by a foreign manufacturer, providing online version, extended version, desktop and plug-in versions. Once you sign up for an account for free, you can edit the content online by creating or uploading a local document. The whole page is refreshing and simple, and you can get enjoyable English experience there. After automatic checking, the problematic words or expressions will be underlined in red. The check includes spelling check, vocabulary check with contextual analysis, grammar check, punctuation check, sentence structure check, etc.

6.6.2 Virtual Writing Tutor

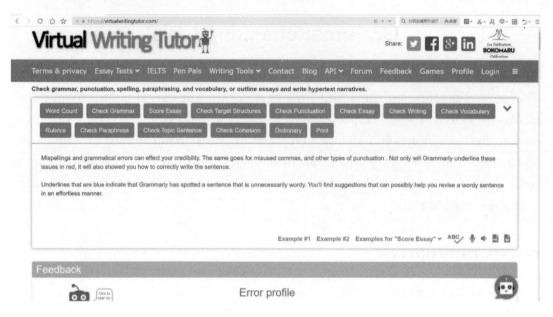

As you can see from the screenshot above, it has various grammar check functions, such as word count, spelling check, grammar check, topic sentence check, dictionary, etc. You just need to copy the text that you need to detect into the text box and then select the features you want.

6.6.3 Hemingway Editor

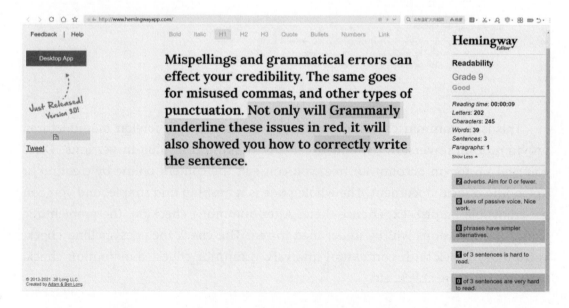

You may wonder whether the English sentences you wrote are authentic or Chinglish. This tool can provide you with a good solution. It can rate the readability of the article, give you alternatives more suitable for the contexts, and remind the users of the changes by different colored highlights.

6.6.4 1Checker

It uses the artificial intelligence technology to help check the text, and can also anticipate what the user wants to express based on the contexts. When words or expressions more suitable for your context are spotted, 1Checker will mark the text, remind you of the inappropriate word usage and provide you with more appropriate substitutes. You can use it for free.

You can have a try after the introduction above and we hope there is one that is suitable for you. You can use them selectively to help check your grammar, make grammatical changes and refine your language.

After-class tasks

❶ Consolidating quizzes

1. **Read the following passage and find out the grammatical characteristics that have been mentioned in this unit.**

What they found is that the initial back-and-forth motion from walking forward affects the initial sloshing or displacement of liquid along the side of the cup. The side-to-side or lateral motion of walking affects the liquid oscillations when the motion is close to the natural oscillations that are allowed by the cup dimensions, but these are not as close to the forward-back motions of stepping. The vertical motions do not contribute significantly to the natural oscillations of the liquid in the cup. Surprisingly the natural oscillations of forward stepping motion coincide well with the natural oscillations allowed for common cup dimensions. What does this mean? That walking tends to "pump" the back and forth motion of the liquid in the cup at just the right time so that it increases in height along the cup's side. Eventually it reaches the rim and spills. This result implies we need some new cup designs, or perhaps we shouldn't walk around with our cups!

2. **The following paragraph is taken from one student's paper entitled "An Analysis of Educational Inequality in Yunnan Province". Try to use the grammatical checking tools introduced in this unit to proofread it and then rewrite it to make it more academic.**

China is now accomplishing the goal of nine-year compulsory education in a planned and systematic way. Universal education, means 85 percent aged children could receive nine-year education. Yunnan Province the rural the minority ares and the eastern coastal inland advanced developed areas of China in compulsory educational development difference is a present-day hot spot problems of both old and new issue. According to official report, Yunnan province basically made nine-year compulsory education universal by the end of 2009, but in reality, education for female children is a problem that must be solved in the popularization of "Nine-year Compulsory Education" in the distresses ethnic minority areas in Yunnan province.

3. **Critical thinking: Between English and Chinese there are many differences in terms of grammatical rules. These differences result from the differences of the thinking modes in different cultures. Can you name some of the differences and analyze the thinking mode behind the specific culture?**

(Points for references: thinking mode is the core of the traditional culture; the experience-oriented synthetic thinking; the logical analytic thinking; the ambiguity of the Chinese language)

Ⅱ Mindmap

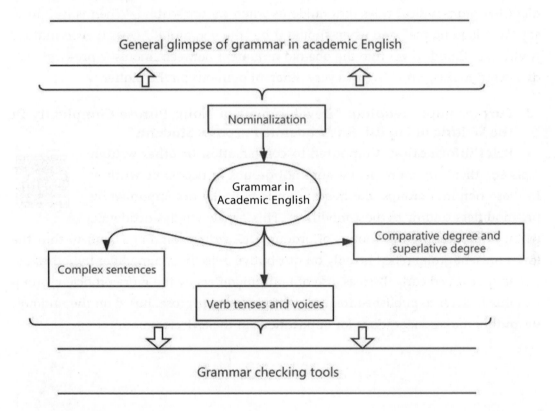

Ⅲ Project task

Till now you may begin to write the first draft of your research paper. When you finish it, please revise it according to the following sub-tasks.

- Use the grammar checking tools to revise the draft;

- Check the verb tenses and voices used in the draft and make corrections if necessary;
- Use nominalization to rewrite the sentences if necessary;
- Change simple sentences into complex ones if necessary.

Each student needs to submit the revised research paper.

Ⅳ Extended resources

1. **TEDEd lesson given by Andreea S. Calude: "Does Grammar Matter?"**

Brief information: It can be hard sometimes, when speaking, to remember all of the grammatical rules that guide us when we are writing. When is it right to say "the dog and me" and when should it be "the dog and I"? Does it even matter? Andreea S. Calude dives into the age-old argument between linguistic prescriptivists and descriptivists, who have two very different opinions on the matter.

2. **Further paper reading: "Development of Noun Phrase Complexity in the Writing of English for Academic Purposes Students"**

Brief information: Compared to conversation or other written registers, there are more heavy nominal groups in academic writing. In these nominal groups, the head noun is typically accompanied by pre-modifiers and/or by post-modifiers. This article studies academic writing produced by two groups of graduate L2 writers. Findings confirm that the less proficient group relied heavily on attributive adjectives, a modifier hypothesized as being acquired early. Besides, use of noun modifiers by the more proficient group was much closer to published frequencies for academic prose. Based on the findings, the author makes suggestions for applications in the EAP classroom.

Unit 7

Translation of English for Science and Technology (EST)

It's widely acknowledged that translation has played a major role in dissemination of knowledge, often scientific or technical, throughout the age. Scientific and technical texts are now increasingly written with international consumption in mind and in English. The binominal phrase "science and technology" occurs frequently in corpora of news and academic prose and it is perhaps its familiar nature that leads us very readily to use the term "scientific and technical translation", which is a complex activity that involves communicating specialized information on a variety of subjects across multiple languages. In practice, it's not unusual for the term "technical translation" to be used to refer to the translation of texts from domains other than technology or applied sciences. Technical translation activity is flourishing in today's global economy and information society in which there is strong demand for product specification instructions, leaflets, user guides, etc., in many languages as well as for the localization of software application. What's more, technical translation encompasses the translation of special language texts, i.e., texts written using languages for special purposes (LSP). As such, technical translation includes not only the translation of texts in engineering or medicine, but also in such disciplines as economics, psychology and law. Translating these texts requires not only a firm mastery of both the source and target languages, but also a good understanding of the subject field, coupled with the research skills needed to write like an expert on the leading edge of technical disciplines.

In this unit, we will introduce translation of English for science and technology from the lexical and syntactic levels to equip students with the knowledge and skills needed in translation and help them understand scientific and technical texts.

Pre-class tasks

❶ Suggested MOOC resources

You can scan the QR code to get features and skills of translation of English for Science and technology.

- Translation skills of terminology
- Translation skills of the passive voice
- Translation skills of attributive clauses
- Translation skills of adverbial clauses

❷ Pre-quizzes

Directions: *Read the following sentences and translate the expressions in bold into Chinese.*

(1) Chinese scientists have created the world's first integrated **space-to-ground quantum network** that can provide reliable, **ultrasecure communication** between more than 150 users over a total distance of 4,600 kilometers across the country, according to a study published in the journal *Nature* on Jan. 7, 2021.

(2) With China already committing to **peak carbon dioxide emissions** before 2030 and achieve **carbon neutrality** before 2060, the Central Economic Work Conference urged quicker steps to come up with an action plan that enables the peaking of emissions. It called for accelerated efforts to better the industry and energy structures and enable the peaking of coal consumption at an early date while bolstering the development of new energy.

(3) China made remarkable progress on **the green governance of express packaging** in 2019, with a more environmentally-friendly development framework taking shape, according to a recent report on the green development of China's post and express industry. Compiled by the development and research center of the State Post Bureau, the report reaffirmed the country's plan to cease the use of non-degradable plastic packaging, plastic tape, and single-use plastic woven bags at postal and express service outlets by 2025.

Expressions	Chinese meanings
space-to-ground quantum network	
ultrasecure communication	
peak carbon dioxide emissions	
carbon neutrality	
the green governance of express packaging	

In-class tasks

7.1
General glimpse of translation of EST

English for science and technology is one kind of English for specific purposes (ESP). EST describes scientific and technical matters. It is a quick and convenient means of communication to exchange news, information or ideas on science and technology. EST was first established and developed in the United Kingdom in the middle of the 20th century. EST research centers had been set up in the United Kingdom and some Western European countries by 1980s. EST, as an independent subject or discipline, has been developed since 1980s in China. And nowadays, it has evolved into its own distinctive features in style, vocabulary and linguistic rules.

EST focuses on texts that are typically translated in scientific and technical domains, such as technical instructions, data sheets and brochures, patents, scientific research articles and abstracts, popular science press releases and news reports. Generally speaking, the stylistic characteristics of English for science and technology can be summarized as follows: objective in statement, strict in logic, standard in language, formal in mode of speech, and concentrated in technical terms. To be specific, there are more professional terms and vocabularies with specifically concentrated meaning, and much more flexible word formations and specialization of everyday words.

7.1.1 Classifications of EST vocabulary

EST exhibits its own various lexical features. It is generally accepted that EST vocabulary can be divided into three categories: technical words, semi-technical words, and non-technical words, including functional words.

7.1.1.1 Technical words

Words used in technical language present the first obstacle to those who have little or no specific knowledge in the related field. Technical words are highly specialized vocabularies with precise narrow meaning used for a given scientific discipline. They denote the phenomena, processes, characteristics, relations, states, amounts, degrees, etc. In the field of science and technology, every subject has its own set of highly technical terms which are an intrinsic part of learning of the discipline itself. The following are some examples.

Technical words	
EST vocabulary	Chinese meanings
hydroxide	氢氧化物
diode	二极管
chromosome	染色体
photon	光子
isotope	同位素

7.1.1.2 Semi-technical words

Semi-technical words are defined as context-independent words which occur with high frequency across disciplines. They can be seen both in EST and general English. However, the meanings of these words in EST are likely to differ from their non-technical meanings. Although they are common in all scientific disciplines, they may have different precise meanings in different technical fields. These words have more different meanings in EST than in general English. The following are some examples.

Semi-technical word: power	
Technical fields	Chinese meanings
General English	权力；能力；力量；国家政权
Mathematics	幂；乘方
Physics	功率
Photology	放大率；焦强
Mechanology	机械工具
Statistics	功效
Electricity	电力；动力
Chemistry	价

In-class exercise 1:

Directions: *Write down the Chinese meanings of "transmission" in different technical fields.*

Semi-technical word: transmission	
Technical fields	Chinese meanings
General English	
Electrical engineering	
Radio engineering	
Mechanical engineering	
Physics	
Medical science	

In-class exercise 2:

Directions: *Write down the Chinese meanings of "carrier" in different technical fields.*

Semi-technical word: carrier	
Technical fields	Chinese meanings
Military science	
Post services	
Chemistry	
Transportation industry	
Medicine and pharmacology	
Car manufacture	
Mechanical engineering	
Radio engineering	

7.1.1.3 Non-technical words

Non-technical words in EST refer to those major terms used in written form with more syllables and are generally much more formal. On the one hand, as EST is a formal written style, formal words are preferred; colloquial, spoken words and slang rarely occurred. On the other hand, scientists and engineers are likely to substitute less technical verbs or phrases for one-word equivalents.

General English words or phrases	Formal expressions in EST
about	concerning/regarding
because	as a consequence of / based on the fact
before	prior to
build	construct
but	however
buy	purchase
change	convert
enlarge	magnify

(Continued)

General English words or phrases	Formal expressions in EST
extra	additional
feeling	sentiment
get	acquire
help	assist
lively	vigorous
many	numerous
not as good as	inferior
quickly	at a high rate
raise	elevate
rest	remainder
some	certain
try	attempt
usually	as a general rule / more often than not / in most cases

General English words or phrases	One-word equivalents in EST
break down / break up	decompose
come from	derive
find out	discover/determine
get away	escape
give off	emit
grow longer	lengthen
hang about	suspend
make neutral	neutralize
pass on	transmit

(Continued)

General English words or phrases	One-word equivalents in EST
pass through	penetrate
put back	replace
put in	insert
put together	aggregate
set fire to	ignite

In-class exercise 3:

Directions: *Write down the formal equivalents for the given expressions.*

General English words or phrases	EST
begin/start	
better than	
can	
do	
expect	
far away	
grow	
more than	
much	
often	
old	
same	
show	
so	
stress/emphasize	
stop	

(Continued)

General English words or phrases	EST
today	
use	
very small	
while	
without	

In-class exercise 4:

Directions: *Write down the one-word equivalents for the given phrasal verbs.*

General English	EST
burn up / use up	
come out	
get rid of	
join together	
look at	
push aside	
push away	
put out	
speed up	
stay alive	
take in	
take out	
use up	
throw back	

Apart from technical words, semi-technical words, and non-technical words in EST, which are highly specialized in meaning with rapid development of science and technology, new terms are needed to define new phenomena and to explain new things and processes. Some suitable terms often have to be invented. Scientists have been extending vocabulary of their subjects for centuries and each subject has its own store of terms with precise and narrow meanings. For example:

New terms	Chinese meanings
webify	使万维网化
webmaster	网络管理员
website	网站
webTV	网络电视
webcasting	网路广播
webliography	网络文件目录

In-class exercise 5:

Directions: Write down the Chinese meanings of the following new terms.

New terms	Chinese meanings
cyberspace	
cybersquatting	
nethead	
cybernut	
netizen	
cyberian	
cybernaut	
cyberphobia	
cyberize	
cybersurf	

7.1.2 Formations of EST vocabulary

7.1.2.1 Compound or composition

A special feature of EST vocabulary is a complex of noun modifiers placed in the front position of the head noun, like "moonwalk", "black hole", "salt-former", etc. A compound is frequently found in technical writing because it shortens the message without obscuring the clarity of the meaning. A compound cannot be grasped in a straight forward way. It is advisable to break it down into some units and interpret them as a postpositional structure. It is also helpful to determine the relations within the compound, namely what modifies what. This structure is very frequently used in EST writing because it is shorter and more direct, and therefore its information is conveyed in a more condensed form. The following are some basic principles on which compound nouns are structured, as well as some examples and their Chinese meanings.

Principles of structuring	Examples	Chinese meanings
principle of operation	friction brake	摩擦制动器
means of operations	foot brake	脚刹车；脚制动器
characteristics of working parts	gear pump	齿轮泵
the person who formulated the operation principle	diesel engine	柴油发动机
materials	glass insulator	玻璃绝缘体
purpose of application	emergency brake	紧急制动器；紧急刹车
location	furnace gases	炉内气体
shape/form	worm gear	蜗轮；螺旋齿；蜗轮蜗杆
professional engagement	air bearing	空气轴承

7.1.2.2 Derivation or affixation

A large portion of English words, especially those used in EST, is formed by adding prefixes and suffixes. We can often detect the meaning of the whole word if we know the meanings of the prefixes. Therefore, knowing the meanings of prefixes and suffixes can help us know the meaning of the words. The following are some examples used in EST.

Prefix (**anti-**)		Suffix (**-ology**)	
EST vocabulary	Chinese meanings	EST vocabulary	Chinese meanings
antibody	抗体	anthro**pology**	人类学
antimatter	反物质	transla**tology**	翻译学
antiproton	反质子	futu**rology**	未来学
antismog	反烟雾	ethnomy**cology**	人种真菌学
antipollution	反污染	esca**pology**	逃生术
antihyperon	反超子	archae**ology**	考古学
anticyclone	反气旋		

7.1.2.3 Blending

Blending is the form of new words by combining parts of two words or a word plus a part of another word. Words formed in this way are called blends or portmanteau words.

Blends	**Chinese meanings**
smog (smoke+fog)	烟雾
medicare (medical+care)	医疗保险
Telex (teleprinter+exchange)	电传
copytron (copy+electron)	电子复写
altiport (altitude+airport)	高山短距离起落机场
lunacast (lunar+telecast)	登月电视广播
chunnel (channel+tunnel)	海峡隧道
advertistics (advertising+statistics)	广告统计学
comsat (communications+satellite)	通信卫星
ballute (balloon+parachute)	减速气球
comint (communication+intelligence)	通信情报
humint (human+intelligence)	间谍情报

(Continued)

Blends	Chinese meanings
Amerind (American+Indian)	美洲印第安人
telediagnosis (television+diagnosis)	远程诊断
carbecue (car+barbeque)	热压熔化废旧汽车的装置
mechanochemistry (mechanical+chemistry)	机械化学

7.1.2.4 Acronym

Another feature of EST vocabulary is the wide use of abbreviations to meet the requirements of conciseness and economy in EST. An acronym is an abbreviation consisting of the initial letters of each word in a technical term, and some can be pronounced as a word.

	Acronyms	Full names	Chinese meanings
Some words are pronounced as the spellings indicate.	SARS	severe acute respiratory syndrome	非典型肺炎（严重急性呼吸综合征）
	MOP	Manned Orbital Platform	载人轨道平台
The string of letters is not easily pronounced as a word, so we can just spell each letter.	DC	direct current	直流电
	DV	digital video	数码摄像机
	UV	ultraviolet	紫外线
	PLC	Programming Logic Control	可编程逻辑控制
The same acronym different meanings in specific fields.	AS	air scoop	空气收集器
	AS	air speed	气流速率
	AS	air station	飞机场
	AS	automatic synchronizer	自动同步器

In-class exercise 6:

Directions: *Write down the Chinese meanings in specific fields in which the acronym is used.*

Acronyms	Full names	Chinese meanings
IC	integrated circuit	
IC	instruction code	
IC	interior communications	
IC	ionization chamber	

7.1.2.5 Clipping

Clipping is the word formation process which consists of the reduction of a word to one of its parts. Clipping is also known as "truncation" or "shortening", and the following are some examples.

Clippings	Original forms
lab	laboratory
gas	gasoline
flu	influenza
cub	cubic
uni	uniform
kilo	kilogram
metro	metrology
math	mathematics

7.1.2.6 Metaphoring

Metaphoring is the way to use a word or phrase in an imaginative way to denote one kind of object or action used in place of another to suggest a likeness and to make the description more powerful. In other words, metaphoring contains an implied comparison in which a word or phrase, ordinarily and primarily used for one thing, is applied to another. The following examples reflect this way of word formation.

EST expressions	Chinese meanings
arm crane	悬臂起重机
bridge crane	桥式起重机；桥式吊车
cable crane	缆索起重机
pillar/column crane	塔式起重机
loading crane	装载起重机；装载吊车
gooseneck crane	鹅颈式起重机
kangaroo grabbing crane	袋鼠抓斗起重机

In-class exercise 7:

Directions: *Write down the Chinese meanings of the following EST expressions by using metaphoring method.*

EST expressions	Chinese meanings
adjustable dog	
stop dog	
locking dog	
watch dog	

7.1.2.7 Analogy-making

Analogy-making has to do with comparison of things based on those things being alike in some way. For example, one can make an analogy between the seasons of the year and the stages of life. Analogy presupposes a model and the regular imitation of a model. It always utilizes old materials for innovations. For example, there are several words in computer science, like "menu", "windows", "mouse", "desktop", "memory", "databank", "host", "port", "electronic mail", etc.

In-class exercise 8:

Directions: *Translate the following expressions into Chinese by using analogy-making method.*

EST expressions	Chinese meanings
sound wave	
light wave	
radio wave	
electromagnetic wave	
microwave	
ultrasonic wave	

7.1.3 Ways to translate EST vocabularies

According to classifications and formations of EST vocabularies, different ways will be adopted while you translate them. The following ways are often used.

Ways of translating	Examples
Transliteration	Hertz（频率）, nylon（尼龙）
Combining phonetic and meaning	sonar pinger system（声呐脉冲测距系统）, carbine（卡宾枪）
Borrowing of images	V-belt（三角皮带）, Cross bit（十字钻头）
Borrowing of lexical items for products, names and models	Steel C-Mn (C-Mn 钢), resolin dye（雷索林染料）
Literal translation	Microsoft（微软）, air-conditioner（空调）
Free translation for proper names with annotations	Alfven wave（阿尔文波）(a magneto hydrodynamics wave discovered by the Swedish scholar Alfven), Kuru（库鲁癫痫症）(from Kurn Highlands)

Sometimes, different ways can be used to translate the same words.

Words	Free translation	Transliteration
engine	发动机	引擎
microphone	传声器	麦克风
combine	联合收割机	康拜因
Vitamin	维生素	维他命

7.1.4 Criteria for EST translation

7.1.4.1 Accuracy

Accuracy means that you should be faithful to the content and information on the basis of a good understanding of the source text (ST) during EST translation, which should be in conformity with the expressing habits in the target language.

> ST: We shall mention here two **temperature scales**, namely, the Fahrenheit scale and the Centigrade scale.
> TV1 (Translated version 1):这里我们将提及两种温度计：华氏表和摄氏表。
> TV2 (Translated version 2):这里我们将提及两种**温标**：华氏**温标**和摄氏**温标**。
> TV2 is more accurate than TV1. In English, "temperature scales" is regarded as a unit of measurement, and the proper Chinese equivalent is "温标", not "温度计", whose English equivalent is "thermometer".

> ST: **Electric machines** are operated until failure occurs.
> TV1: 电机在发生损坏以前一直运行着。
> TV2: 在出现故障之前**电机设备**一直运行正常。

TV2 is more accurate than TV1. In Chinese "电机" is a technical word, having both a special meaning of generator or electric motor and an extensive meaning of any power-generating or power-driven machine and of electrical machinery in the professional field of electricity industry. Therefore, "electric machines" in the ST should imply the meaning in an extensive way and be translated into "电机设备".

7.1.4.2 Expressiveness

Expressiveness means that the translation should not only be expressive and easy to understand, but also in conformity with the grammatical structure and expressing habits in the target language, and free from translationese as well.

> ST: Distillation involves heating the solution until water evaporates, and then condensing the vapor.
>
> TV1: 蒸馏就是加热溶液直到水蒸发，然后冷凝蒸汽。
>
> TV2: 蒸馏就是要**把**溶液加热，直到水蒸发，然后再**使**蒸汽冷凝。

To be smooth and easy to understand, it is necessary to add the Chinese " 把 " and " 使 " to make the object of "heat" and "condense" more specific, so TV2 is more expressive.

> ST: Rubber is not hard; it gives way to pressure.
>
> TV1: 橡胶不硬，屈服于压力。
>
> TV2: 橡胶**性软**，**受**压会**变形**。

Obviously, TV2 is more expressive than TV1, without translationese.

7.1.4.3 Conciseness

Conciseness means that the translation should be as brief as possible, keeping away from the use of empty and superfluous words and unnecessary repetitions so as to convey the complete information in the source text effectively and efficiently into the target language.

> ST: **Three of Archimedes' extant works** are **devoted to** plane geometry.
>
> TV1: 阿基米德现存的三部著作都是献给平面几何的。
>
> TV2: 阿基米德现存的**著作中有三本**是**专门论述**平面几何的。

Here, the word "devote" cannot be translated literally into " 献给 " and in Chinese " 专门论述 " is more concise. In addition, it is necessary to distinguish the following two expressions: "three of Archimedes' works" and "**the** three of Archimedes' works".

> ST: 按照传统说法，化学已逐步发展成了四大分支：有机化学、无机化学、物理化学和分析化学。
>
> TV1: According to traditional saying, chemistry has developed into four large/ great branches: organic chemistry, inorganic chemistry, physical chemistry and analytical chemistry.
>
> TV2: Traditionally chemistry has evolved into four provinces: organic, inorganic, physical and analytical chemistry.

Clearly, TV2 is more concise than TV1, without word for word translation.

Bearing the classifications, formations and ways to translate EST vocabularies in mind, we can use different translation skills to meet the above mentioned criteria during the process of EST translation. According to the different features, functions, styles and contexts of EST resources, scholars also summarize the different criteria about EST translation, such as keeping faithful and accurate, smooth and fluent, standard and professional. All in all, a translation should give a complete transcript of the ideas of the original work with all the ease of the original composition.

7.2
Translation of the passive voice in EST

7.2.1 Situations to use passive voice

EST focuses on describing objective facts, expounding the results of science and technology as well as the process of experimental research and data. Therefore, the meaning of sentence will be clearer and those information can be emphasized in the passive voice.

> ST: As oil **is found** deep in the ground, its presence **cannot be determined** by a study of the surface. Consequently, a geological survey of the underground rock structure **must be carried out.**
> TV: 石油**埋藏**于地层深处。因此，仅研究地层表面，无法**确定**有无石油，必须勘察地下的岩石结构。

In the above example, there are only two sentences in which three passive voices "is found", "cannot be determined" and "must be carried out" are used respectively.

In general, the passive voice is always used under the following three situations.

First, the doer of the action is not known.

> ST: The house which is quite old **was built** in 1950.
> TV: 这座很旧的房子**是** 1950 年建造**的**。

Second, do not emphasize the doer of the action.

> ST: Calculator **cannot be used** in the math exam.
> TV: 数学考试**不能使用**计算器。

Third, to avoid mentioning oneself or other people.

> ST: Electricity **is used** to run machines.
> TV: **用**电运行机器。

7.2.2 Ways to translate the passive voice

7.2.2.1 To translate it into the active voice in Chinese

The passive voice can be translated into the active voice in Chinese, and words such as "人们" or "我们" can be added as the subject.

> ST: The mechanism of fever production is not completely understood.
> TV: **人们**还不完全清楚发烧的产生机理。

With the wide application of this structure, below are some expressions widely accepted as conventions with their Chinese meanings.

English expressions	Chinese meanings
It is well known that…	众所周知
It is believed that…	人们相信
It is taken that…	人们认为
It is noted that…	人们注意到；有人指出
It is generally considered that…	人们普遍认为
It is sometimes asked that…	人们有时会问

When the subject of the passive sentence is an inanimate noun, this sentence can be translated into an active sentence.

> ST: That computer is being repaired.
> TV: 那台计算机正在修理。

Some passive sentences can usually be translated into non-subject sentences.

> ST: If water **is heated**, the molecules move very quickly.
> TV: 如果**把**水加热，分子运动就会更快。

The following are some fixed expressions with the passive voice and their Chinese meanings.

English expressions	Chinese meanings
It is found that…	据发现
It is said that…	据说
It is reported that…	据报道
It is illustrated that…	据图示；据说明
It must be admitted that…	必须承认
It must be pointed out that…	必须指出
It will be seen from this that…	由此可见
It was estimated that…	据估计

The passive voice can be translated into the active voice in Chinese, and the action of the doer guided by *by* can be translated as the subject.

> ST: Hate and light are given off **by the chemical reaction**.
> TV: **这种化学反应**能发出热和光。

Some sentences in the passive voice can be translated into the active voice in Chinese, and the adverbial can be translated as the subject.

> ST: The newly-found building material is widely used **home and abroad**.
> TV: **国内外**广泛采用这种新型建筑材料。

Some sentences in the passive voice can be translated into the active voice in Chinese by translating the subject-predicate structure in the passive sentence into nominal structure.

> ST: **Instructions are executed** in the sequence they are stored in memory.
> TV: **指令的执行**是按照其在存储器中的存储顺序进行的。

With the structure of "sth. A be done to do sth. B", some sentences in the passive voice can be translated into the active voice in Chinese by translating the structure of "sth. A be done" as the subject, while structure of "to do sth. B" as the predicate.

> ST: **A special fund has been set up** to help these nations use new chemicals and technology.
>
> TV: **已经建立了特殊基金**帮助这些国家使用新的化学品和新技术。

7.2.2.2 To translate it into the passive voice in Chinese

Some passive structures can be kept by using the words like "被""由""受到""遭到""得到""予以""加以""为……所""称""让""给""挨""用""靠""通过" and so on during the process of EST translation in order to lay emphasis on the processes and actions.

> ST: With the computer, the ideas of today's scientists **can be** studied, tested, distributed, and used more rapidly than ever before.
>
> TV: 有了计算机，当今科学家们的理论就可以比过去任何时候都更快地**得到**研究、检验、传播及应用。

7.2.2.3 To translate it into declarative sentences in Chinese

Some passive structures, emphasizing on the specific circumstance related to the action, such as time, place, way and method but not the action itself, can be translated into declarative sentences by using the structure of "是……的" or "……的是……".

> - ST: Hydrogen **is known** to be the lightest element.
>   TV: 人们知道，氢**是**最轻**的**元素。
> - ST: Currently most solar cells **are made** from crystals of high-purity silicon.
>   TV: 目前，绝大多数太阳能电池**是**用高纯度的硅晶体制成**的**。

7.2.2.4 To translate it into sentences with no subjects in Chinese

When the passive voice sentences are used to describe the occurrence, existence and disappearance of the events, express the opinions, attitudes, warnings and requirements, or state scientific facts, scientific process and ethics of science, they can be translated into sentences with no subjects by adding the Chinese characters "把"

"使""将""对" and so on.

> ST: Mechanical energy can **be changed** into electrical energy by a generator.
> TV: 发电机可以**将**机械能变为电能。

7.2.2.5 To translate it into the sentence with the Chinese character "把"

The sentence with Chinese character "把" is a unique sentence pattern in Chinese. In the translation of some English passive sentences (no matter whether there is a *by*-guide phrase), the Chinese character "把" can be placed before the subject of the original sentence, that is, the subject of the original English passive sentence is translated into the object of the Chinese character "把", and the whole sentence into this pattern with Chinese character "把".

> ST: All the sounds **are fed into** a computer and analyzed.
> TV: **把**所有的声音输进计算机进行分析。

Some passive structures can be translated into the "把" sentence pattern in Chinese, and the noun after *by* can be translated into the subject, omitting *by*.

> ST: Machine parts of irregular shape can **be washed** very clean by ultrasonic waves.
> TV: 超声波**能把**形状不规则的机件冲**洗得**干干净净。

To sum up, the translation methods above can be often used for dealing with the passive voice during the process of EST translation, and we need to apply them carefully and properly.

7.3

Translation of attributive clauses in EST

Attributive clauses are often used in EST to define, describe, explain, identify things or add extra information. According to the types of attributive clauses and whether they are guided by *as*, we will adopt different ways to translate attributive clauses in EST.

7.3.1 Types of attributive clauses

A restrictive attributive clause identities or classifies a noun or pronoun in the main clause, while a non-restrictive attributive clause adds extra information about a noun or pronoun in the main clause, and sometimes even about the main clause.

Introducers	Used for	Used as			
Pronouns		Subject	Object	Restrictive	Non-restrictive
who	people, animals	√	√	√	√
whom	people	×	√	√	√
which	objects, animals, ideas	√	√	√	√
that	people, animals, ideas	√	√	√	×
whose	relationships, possessions	×	×	√	√
Adverbs					
where	places	×	×	√	√
when	time	×	×	√	√
why	reasons	×	×	√	√

From the table above, you may get a clear understanding of the antecedents, the introducers, their functions in an attributive clause and the types of attributive clauses.

7.3.2 Ways to translate attributive clauses

7.3.2.1 Inversion

In EST, attributive clauses always come after the antecedents while in Chinese they are always before the modified nouns or pronouns. During the EST translation process, if they are a little bit short, they may be translated into Chinese by using inversion.

• ST: "Parallel" is used here to refer to straight lines, the distance between **which**

remains the same.
TV: 这里我们把"平行"这个词用来指**其间隔距离保持相同的**两条直线。

- ST: Engineering design is a decision-making process used for the development of engineering **for which there is a human need.**
TV: 工程设计是**为发展人类所需**工程而做决定的工程。

From the two examples above, you may notice that in EST, if an attributive clause is short, it may be good to utilize inversion to realize the idiomatic expression in Chinese.

7.3.2.2 Combination

In EST, sometimes an attributive clause can be translated into an independent sentence by integrating the subject of the attributive clause with that of the main clause or the antecedence due to the close relationship between the attributive clause and the main clause. The structure "……的" will usually be adopted in the Chinese version.

- ST: The rate **at which the molecules move** depends upon the energy **they have.**
TV: **分子运动的**速率取决于分子**所具有的**能量。
- ST: People **who live in the areas where earthquakes are a common occurrence** should build houses **that are resistant to ground movement.**
TV: **居住在地震多发地区的**人们应该建造**能抗震的**房屋。

7.3.2.3 Division

Division means that in the translation of EST, some attributive clauses can be separated from their antecedents and translated into an independent sentence in Chinese. Non-restrictive attributive clauses, attributive clauses describing the whole sentences, and longer restrictive relative clauses can be translated into parallel clauses depending on the context by adopting the following ways: repeating the antecedent, repeating the antecedent and adding an adversative, omitting the antecedent.

- ST: This is a college of science and technology, the students **of which are trained to be engineers or scientists.**
TV: 这是一所科技大学，**该校**学生将被培养成工程师或科学工作者。
- ST: Each of our faculty focuses on understanding the basic chemical, physical and biological phenomenon **that underlines an engineering research problem**

> **under consideration.**
> TV: 我们每一位教师都关注基本的化学、物理和生物现象，**而这些现象**是当前研究工程问题的基础。
> - ST: The lungs are subject to several diseases **which are treatable by surgery.**
> TV: 肺易受几种疾病的侵袭，但均可进行手术治疗。

7.3.2.4 Conversion

In EST, some attributive clauses may sometimes contain the meaning of such logic relationship as reason, time, result and condition, etc. These attributive clauses can be translated into Chinese by converting into corresponding adverbial clauses. The method of conversion is adopted to convey the original meaning in the source text accurately.

1. To convert into the predicate

The predicate of the clause can be converted into the predicate of the main sentence. In the "there be…" structure, the subject is mostly a noun with a restrictive attributive clause, the core meaning of the sentence, which is often converted into the predicate of the main sentence in Chinese.

> ST: There are some metals **that possess the power to conduct electricity and the ability to be magnetized.**
> TV: 有些金属**具有**导电能力和磁化能力。

2. To convert into an appositive

When the attributive clause is a simple verb + complement, the predicate part can be converted into an appositive.

> ST: Hydrogen, **which is the lightest element,** has only one electron.
> TV: **最轻的元素**氢只有一个电子。

3. To convert into the adverbial modifier

The attributive clause can be translated into adverbial clauses to explain the cause, result, purpose, concession, condition, time, etc.

> - ST: A solid fuel, like coal or wood, can only burn at the surface, **where it comes into contact with the air.**

TV: 固体燃料，如煤和木材，只能在表面燃烧，**因为表面接触空气**。

- ST: The stimulation of nerve receptors causes the blood vessels (by reflex action) to dilate, **which also facilitates blood flow.**

  TV: 对神经受体的刺激使得血管（通过反射作用）扩张，**从而又有利于血流运动**。

- ST: A body **that contains only atoms with the same general properties** is called an element.

  TV: 物质**如果包含的原子性质都相同**，则称之为元素。

- ST: In general, steam-operated electric power plants are located by rivers **where barges can easily bring in the coal that the power plants consume each day.**

  TV: 一般来说，热电厂都设在河边，**以便驳船把发电厂用的煤运来**。

- ST: Anyone **who has tugged heavy hand baggage down endless airport corridors, or waited for delayed flight in a sterile lounge** will know how user-unfriendly many airports are in design terms.

  TV: 任何人**当他拖着沉重的随身行李，走过无止境的机场走廊，或者在枯燥乏味的休息室里等候延误的班机时**，他都会体会到许多机场在设计上对旅客是多么的不方便。

- ST: Electronic computers, **which have many advantages**, cannot carry out creative work and replace man.

  TV: **虽然电子计算机有很多优点**，但他们不能进行创造性的工作，也代替不了人。

7.3.2.5 Annotation

When the non-restrictive attributive clause plays a supplementary explanatory role, annotation can be used for translation.

- ST: To take away the refining part of the steel making cycle off an electric arc furnace, **which is discussed elsewhere**, is an excellent start.

  TV: 把炼钢周期中的精炼阶段从电弧炉中移走（**这个问题将在别处加以讨论**），是一个良好的开端。

7.3.3 Ways to translate attributive clauses guided by *as*

1. The structure "such+ (noun)+ as / such as" can be translated into "像……之类的""像……（这）那样的""……的一种"

- ST: **Such liquid fuel rockets as** are now being used for space research have to carry their own supply of oxygen.

> TV: **像**现在用于宇宙研究的**这类**液态燃料火箭，必须自带氧气。

2. The structure "the same...as" can be translated into "和……一样" "与……相同的"

> • ST: Many inventors followed **the same principles as** French inventor had used in his invention.
> TV: 许多发明家遵循那个法国发明家在他的发明中曾用过**的同样**原理进行发明创造。

In most cases, the negative meaning of the main clause can be transferred to the attributive clause led by *as* in a negative sentence. In this situation, the attributive clause can be translated into "与……相反" or "主句主语+并不像……那样".

> • ST: Spiders are not insects, **as many people think**, nor even related to them.
> TV1: **与许多人所想的相反**，蜘蛛并不属于昆虫类，甚至与昆虫没有近亲关系。
> TV2: 蜘蛛**并不像**许多人所想的**那样**属于昆虫类，它甚至与昆虫没有近亲关系。
> • ST: The Earth does not move round in the empty space **as it was once thought to be**.
> TV1: **与人们曾经认为的相反**，地球并不是在空无一物的空间中运转的。
> TV2: 地球**并不像**人们曾经认为的**那样**是在空无一物的空间中运转的

When the attributive clause introduced by *as* is at the beginning of a sentence, and *as* is the subject of the clause, the negative meaning cannot be transferred.

> • ST: **As is known to all**, man can't live without air.
> TV: 众所周知，**没有**空气人就**不能**生存。
> • ST: **As is very natural**, a body at rest will not move unless it is acted upon by a force.
> TV: 静止的物体**没有**外力作用，就**不会**移动，这是很自然的。

To sum up, during the process of EST translation, we need to clearly understand the logic relationship of the main clause and the attributive clause and choose proper translation methods to handle the attributive clauses in the source text.

7.4

Translation of adverbial clauses in EST

Adverbial clauses are widely used in EST to add a modifier and express an idea much more clearly.

7.4.1 Types of adverbial clauses

English adverbial clauses can be divided into nine types on the basis of their different functions, and they are:

- The adverbial clause of time
- The adverbial clause of condition
- The adverbial clause of purpose
- The adverbial clause of reason
- The adverbial clause of concession
- The adverbial clause of place
- The adverbial clause of comparison
- The adverbial clause of manner
- The adverbial clause of result

From the following table, you can clearly see the types, common conjunctions, functions and examples of these nine adverbial clauses.

Nine types of adverbial clauses			
Types of clauses	Common conjunctions	Functions	Examples
time	when, before, after, since, while, as, as long as, till, until, etc.; hardly...when, scarcely...when, barely...when, no sooner...than	to show the time something happens	• Her goldfish died *when she was young.* • He came *after night had fallen.* • We *barely* had gotten there *when mighty Casey struck out.*

(Continued)

Nine types of adverbial clauses			
Types of clauses	Common conjunctions	Functions	Examples
condition	if, unless, lest	to talk about a possible or counterfactual situation and its consequences	• *If they lose weight during an illness*, they soon regain it afterwards.
purpose	in order to, so that, in order that, in case	to indicate the purpose of an action	• They had to take some of his land *so that they could extend the churchyard*.
reason	because, since, as, given	to indicate the reason for something	• I couldn't feel anger against him *because I liked him too much*.
concession	although, though, while, but	to show contrasts with others or make something seem surprising	• I used to read a lot *although I don't get much time for books now*.
place	where, wherever, anywhere, everywhere, etc.	to talk about the location or position of something	• He said he was happy *where he was*.
comparison	as...as, than, as	to show comparison of a skill, size or amount, etc.	• You should run *as fast as you can*.
manner	as, like, the way	to talk about someone's behavior or the way something is done	• I was never allowed to do things *as I wanted to do them*.

(Continued)

Nine types of adverbial clauses			
Types of clauses	Common conjunctions	Functions	Examples
result	so...that, such...that	to indicate the result(s) of an act or event	• My suitcase had become *so* damaged *that the lid would not stay closed.*

7.4.2 Ways to translate adverbial clauses

7.4.2.1 Sequence

When the adverbial clause is at the beginning of a sentence showing time, place, purpose, reason, condition, concession, etc., it is very common to use the translation method of sequence.

- ST: **Whenever a wave moves out from a source in uniform medium**, it travels in straight lines.
  TV: **每当**波从均匀介质中的波源发出时，它都呈直线传播。
- ST: All living things, **whether they are animals or plants**, are made up of cells.
  TV: 一切生物，**不管**是动物还是植物，都是由细胞组成的。

7.4.2.2 Inversion

In EST, the word order of most sentences is mainly on the contrary to that in Chinese. In this case, the EST translation into Chinese can be finished by inversion, i.e., inverting the original order of the sentences in the source text to conform to the habitual Chinese expression. Inversion is usually adopted when the adverbial clauses of the time, concession, manner, purpose, and reason are at the end.

- ST: The piston completes a stroke **each time it changes direction of motion.**
  TV: 活塞**每改变一次运动方向**就完成了一个冲程。
- ST: The ends of the wires are soldered **so as not to fray during vibration.**
  TV: **为了避免震动时磨损**，线头要焊牢。

7.4.2.3 Conversion

In EST, some adverbial clauses of time and those of place may sometimes contain the meaning of condition, reason or other subordinate relationships. When translating these sentences, we may utilize the method of conversion, otherwise we may not correctly present the original meaning.

- ST: The materials are excellent for use **where the value of the work pieces is not high.**
  TV: **如果零件价值不高，**最好使用这种材料。
- ST: Cracks will come out clean **when they are treated by ultrasonic waves.**
  TV: **如果用超声波处理，**缝隙就会变得很干净。
  The short adverbial clause can be translated into a compound sentence without transitional words, which can make the Chinese sentence more compact and concise.
- ST: The vapor pressure of water increases **as the temperature is raised.**
  TV: **温度升高，**水的蒸汽压也升高。
- ST: **When atoms split**, the process is called fission.
  TV: **原子分裂，**其过程被称为裂变。

7.4.2.4 Division

In EST, some sentences are usually very complex, in which the adverbial clause can be separated from the main clause, thus can be translated into an independent sentence in Chinese. In this case, division is used for the EST translation into Chinese.

- ST: Never get on or off the bus **before it comes to a standstill.**
  TV: **车未停稳，**切勿上下。
- ST: It is frequently said that computers solve problems **only because they are "programmed" to do so.**
  TV: 人们常说，电脑之所以能解决问题，**只是因为电脑输入了解决问题的"程序"。**

7.4.2.5 Combination

In EST, some compound sentences containing adverbial clauses can be translated into a simple sentence by omitting either the subject of the main clause or that of the adverbial clause, as they are in fact the same one. In this case, combination is adopted for the EST translation into Chinese.

> • ST: Seawater can be used for a supply of drinkable water **if it can be separated from the salt dissolved in it.**
>   TV: 海水**把其中的盐分离出去**就可用作饮用水。
> • ST: Atoms are so small **that they cannot be seen at all with the naked eyes.**
>   TV: 原子小得**用肉眼根本看不到**。

To sum up, the methods above can be mainly used in the translation of the adverbial clauses in EST.

What's more, to be a qualified scientific translator, there are some requirements:

- Having a broad knowledge of the subjects involved;
- Being capable of employing translating skills involved in translation of EST;
- Having a full understand of the technical terms;
- Being familiar with sentence structures frequently used in EST;
- Being able to analyze the deep structures profoundly;
- Having a good command of English and Chinese;
- Being rigorous.

7.5
Think-pair-share activity

Directions: Read the following paragraph and pay attention to the expressions in bold. Try to replace the expressions with formal ones. Discuss your understanding of this paragraph with a partner and exchange your thoughts. Then rewrite the paragraph into a formal one and translate it into Chinese. Finally, share your version in the class.

> People **get** natural rubber from rubber trees as a white, milky liquid, **which is called** latex. They **mix it with** acid, and dry it, **and then they send it** to countries all over the world. As the rubber industry **grew**, people **needed** more and more rubber. They started rubber plantations in countries with hot, **wet weather conditions**, but these still could not **give enough** raw rubber to **meet the needs** of the growing industry.

Graphic Organizer

Expressions	What I thought	What my partner thought	What we will share
get			
which is called			
mix it with			
and then they send it			
grew			
needed			
wet weather conditions			
give enough			
meet the needs			

My name: Partner's name: Date:

After-class tasks

❶ Consolidating quizzes

1. Translate the following EST expressions into Chinese and identify their ways of word formation.

EST expressions	Chinese meanings	Ways of word formation
hydrophobic		
telex		
insulating material		
math		
ecocide		

(Continued)

EST expressions	Chinese meanings	Ways of word formation
interplanetary		
COVID-19		
carrier transmission		
thermodynamics		
bridge crane		

2. **Translate the English sentences into Chinese and vice versa.**

(1) Freeing aluminum from its compounds is something very difficult, which accounts for its recent introduction into general use.

(2) We live in an age where voice, data, and video are just bits, ones and zeros.

(3) The amount of work is dependent on the applied force and the distance the body is moved.

(4) This product has been inspected before delivery and is in full conformity with our standard.

(5) The more carbon the steel contains, the harder and stronger it is.

(6) 车未停稳，切勿上下。

(7) 同性电荷相斥，异性电荷相吸。

(8) 防止这种事故发生的办法是使导线完全绝缘。

(9) 因此，当煤堆得太厚，煤在堆里缓慢氧化而产生的热无法散出，就可能引起煤堆自行着火。

(10) 还有一些人建议，通过增强发射到黑洞的无线电波，人类将来有可能利用黑洞制造炸弹。

3. **Critical thinking: With the fast development and wide applications of science and technology, EST translation has been playing an increasingly vital role in academic learning. Scan the QR code to read the passage and share your opinion about the approaches to EST translation with the aid of computer or machine technology.**

(Points for references: computer-aided translation (CAT); machine translation

(MT); a human translator; the responsibility; facilitate; intervention; a continuum of translation possibilities; machine or human assistance)

Ⅱ Mindmap

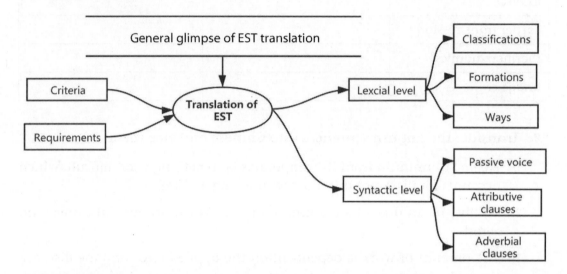

Ⅲ Project task

For this project, you are supposed to translate the abstract of a research article in your major. You can develop your project from the following perspectives:

- Read the abstracts (both English version and Chinese version) of at least three articles with the same key words of the top five journals in your field;
- Explore the linguistic characteristics of the abstracts of research articles;
- Find the differences between English and Chinese versions of the abstracts;
- Translate the abstract of your research article and finalize the version that you will submit for an international conference.

Ⅳ Extended resources

1. TED talk: "Why Translation Is Like Music"

Brief information: Translation is both art and science and the reality is that technology shapes all of the arts, and it's also shaping the way people perform those arts. What does music cost depends on the type of music, and it also depends on how many people are involved in making music. So if you want to know how much you should pay for translation, it really depends on how you want it to sound good; there are translators like the musicians you see in the subway and there are translators like the artists on stage at the symphony. Most translation projects, at least for business purposes, are like a string quartet: Someone does the translation, someone reviews it, someone proof reads it and someone manages the process.

2. Further paper reading: "Study on Features and Translation of New Scientific and Technological Terms"

Brief information: This paper discusses the features and word formation of new scientific and technological terms as well as the principles of translation that should be followed as far as translation of the new items is concerned. The purpose of this paper is to afford a clue on how to understand and use the terms effectively.

References

Campbell, C., & Smith, J. 2015. *English for academic study: Listening*. Beijing: Foreign Language Teaching and Research Press.

Gautham, V. et al. 2020. Enhancement of soot combustion in diesel particulate filters by ceria nanofiber coating. *Applied Nanoscience*, *10*(7): 2429–2438.

Glasman-Deal, H. 2010. *Science research writing for non-native speakers of English*. London: Imperial College Press.

Hurtig, N. C., & William-Jones, A. E. 2014. An experimental study of the transport of gold through hydration of AuCl in aqueous vapor and vapor-like fluids. *Geochimica et Cosmochimica Acta*, *127*: 305–325.

Langan, J., 2018. *College writing skills with readings* (9th edition). Beijing: Foreign Language Teaching and Research Press.

Lebenbaum, M., Laporte, A., & Oliveira, C. 2021. The effect of mental health on social capital: An instrumental variable analysis. *Journal of Social Science and Medicine*, (272): 1–9.

Liu, S. et al. 2021. Measurement of electronic structure and surface reconstruction in the superionic $Cu_{2-x}Te$. *Physical Review*, *103* (11): 1–11.

McCormack, J., & Slaght, J. 2011. *Extended writing & research skills for academic English study*. Beijing: Foreign Language Teaching and Research Press.

Newman, A. J. et al. 2012. The influence of language proficiency on lexical semantic processing in native and late learners of English. *Journal of Cognitive Neuroscience*, *24*(5): 1205–1223.

Nirrengarten, M. et al. 2016. Application of the critical Coulomb wedge theory to hyper-extended, magma-poor rifted margins. *Earth and Planetary Science Letters*, *442*(52): 121–132.

O'Dell, K. et al. 2020. Hazardous air pollutants in fresh and aged Western US wildfire smoke and implications for long-term exposure. *Environmental Science & Technology*, *54*(19): 11838–11847.

Parkinson, J., & Musgrave, J. 2014. Development of noun phrase complexity in the writing of English for Academic Purposes students. *Journal of English for*

Academic Purposes, 14: 48–59.

Purakayastha, T. J., & Chhonkar, P. K. 2009. Phytoremediation of heavy metal contaminated soils. *Soil Biology*, 19: 389–429.

Purnell, B. A. 2021a. Repairing the fish heart. *Science*, *372*(15): 201.

Purnell, B. A. 2021b. Screen identifies demethylation regulator. *Science*, *372*(15): 128.

Rohrbach, N., & Stewart, B. R. 1986. Using microcomputers in teaching. *The Journal of the American Association of Teacher Educators in Agriculture*, *27*(4), 18–25.

Rosenwasser, D., & Stephen, J. 2019. *Writing analytically for Chinese students*. Beijing: Peking University Press.

Smith, K. T. 2021. X-rays from giant radio pulses. *Science*, *372*(15): 187.

Wang, Y. et al. 2021. Maturity and thermal evolution differences between two sets of Lower Palaeozoic shales and its significance for shale gas formation in southwestern Sichuan Basin, China. *Geological Journal*, *56* (7): 1–22.

Weissberg, R., & Buker, S.1990. *Writing up research: Experimental research report writing for students of English*. Englewood Cliffs: Prentice Hall Regents.

Xiong, M. et al. 2020. Human stem cell-derived neurons repair circuits and restore neural function. *Cell Stem Cell*, *28*(1): 1–15.

蔡基刚. 2017. 学术英语：理工. 北京：外语教学与研究出版社.

韩金龙，崔岭. 2018. 新时代大学学术英语综合教程（上册）. 上海：上海外语教育出版社.

季佩英，范烨. 2013. 学术英语：综合. 北京：外语教学与研究出版社.

姜怡，姜欣. 2015. 学术交流英语. 北京：高等教育出版社.

雷秀云. 2020. 基于语料库的学术英语语法的频率特征. 上海交通大学学报（社科版），1（8）：117–119.

秦荻辉. 2007. 科技英语语法. 北京：外语教学与研究出版社.

夏历，郭魏. 2020. 英语学术论文写作改·评·析. 北京：北京航空航天大学出版社.

闫莉，孙洪丽，程文华. 2017. 英语研究论文写作. 上海：上海交通大学出版社.

杨惠中. 2017. 大学学术英语视听说教程. 上海：上海外语教育出版社.